REIGNING IN HIS POWER

Reigning in His Power

A Study on How to *REIN* in the
Power of the *Holy Spirit*
in Your Daily Walk

A JANE BOSTON BIBLE STUDY

www.janeboston.com

Proceeds from this Bible study are designated to help grow
Motivations Ministries ...
Christian Events in Every City
www.motivationsministries.org

WestBow
PRESS
A DIVISION OF THOMAS NELSON

Requests for permission should be addressed to:
Jane Boston: Motivations, Inc., 3581 Centre Circle, Ste 104, Fort Mill, SC 29715.
Electronic requests are accepted: www.janeboston.com

To order additional copies of Reigning in His Power, for instruction or group studies, contact us directly at: Motivations Ministries, Inc., 3581 Centre Circle, Ste 104, Fort Mill, SC 29715. Tel: (803) 802-5454. Or online: www.janeboston.com

WestBow Press books may be ordered through booksellers or by contacting:

WestBow Press
A Division of Thomas Nelson
1663 Liberty Drive
Bloomington, IN 47403
www.westbowpress.com
1-(866) 928-1240

ISBN: 978-1-4497-1124-5 (sc)
ISBN: 978-1-4497-1123-8 (e)

Library of Congress Control Number: 2011920426

This study has been designed & adapted by UPLIFT Publishing Co.
www.encouragethekingdom.com

Cover design consultation: Spark Publications
www.sparkpublications.com

Photo furniture consultation furnished by: London Church Furniture
www.londonchurchfurniture.com

Printed in the United States of America

WestBow Press rev. date: 2/14/2011

INTRODUCTION

Who would believe we have within us the very thoughts and mind of Christ and the power to move the hands of God (1 Cor. 2:16 TLB)? This verse from the Bible offers great insight and clarity into what God intended for those who love Him. The Creator of the universe intended to share Himself with us by offering His power to us through the Holy Spirit. This is the portion of our faith that was meant to move our thoughts directly in line with what God wanted us to do.

How do you rein in the power of the Holy Spirit? This book explores this vague concept in very concrete terms, bringing together Scriptures, real-life experiences, and a passion for knowing when to act and when to wait in God's perfect timing. The power is vital to fulfill the callings placed on our life. Without an understanding of the power, we are powerless to perform.

What kind of power can we receive through the Holy Spirit? Power can bring knowledge, which may just look like wisdom. This result, known in the Bible as prophecy, brings understanding of our mission, our direction, and our purpose. We can receive power to grow the gifts of the spirit and the fruits of a God-loving personality. We can reign in power to perform God's plans, mostly by allowing Him to evolve through us the tasks necessary to complete work in His name. And we can receive power over our emotions to remove stress and replace anxiety with confidence in God's plan to care for us.

How does all this work? In my first professional job as a social worker to very disabled children, for the first time in my life, I wanted the power that I had read about but never understood. The sadness in meeting these children overwhelmed me. I wanted to help by bringing resources to make these children's lives easier. I wanted to comfort their parents, find therapy for the children's pain, furnish wheelchairs, and offer funds. Alone as a young new professional, I was sure that the God of the universe would help me. In my quest, He showed me the power of prayer for the first time. The name of Jesus could deliver, sometimes in hours, what my hard-working self might toil over for weeks.

As my career responsibilities in administration grew, my heart found more and more ways to seek God's resources for disabled persons. During that time, God would call me to build a $3.7 million new rehab facility, manage a $7 million annual budget, and oversee 250 employees. These were large tasks by the world's standards but small to God's vast power and abilities. After years of sitting in church programs growing up, I was starting to get it. God could and would deliver if I prayed it into happening. By the end of a nineteen-year career in agencies for disabled persons, God showed me how to work smarter, not harder. His hand could be moved. My heart would be changed.

My career would move forward to building a national continuing education company for medical rehab professionals. In just three years, without obvious funding, this would become a million-dollar business by walking it out God's way.

God reigns. Most believers understand and accept that. The less-discussed concept is in understanding how to rein in His power to fulfill our callings, enhance our personalities, and walk it out stress free. During the birth and near death of our only child, God spared our son's life. In that experience, God brought me to a higher calling to no longer be quiet about how one can rein in God's power.

This Bible study shares the passion for how to find, implement, and rejoice in the power of the Holy Spirit. There is no reason not to speak of this biblical concept. God is glorified in sharing His power with His believers. May this Bible study open doors to take your daily walk to the next level of action toward the final end of bringing more souls to heaven.

Jane Boston, Author and Speaker
www.janeboston.com

OUTLINE

I. Understanding His Master Plan

Week 1   The Mission Statement 1

Week 2   Making It Look Appealing 11

Week 3   Understanding the Will of God 17

II. Preparing Ourselves To Serve

Week 4   Christ's Perfect Love 25

Week 5   Gaining Peace 29

Week 6   Building Integrity 39

III. Learning To Listen

Week 7   Believing Him for Direction 51

Week 8   Recognizing His Voice 61

Week 9   Growing in Clarity 75

IV. Acting in His Perfect Timing

Week 10   Praying Efficiently 87

Week 11   Discerning His Will 93

V. Working in Rhythm with the Master

Week 12   Exciting Assignments 103

Week 13   Friends in High Places 113

I. UNDERSTANDING HIS MASTER PLAN

Week 1   The Mission Statement........................1

Week 2   Making It Look Appealing 11

Week 3   Understanding the Will of God 17

THE MISSION STATEMENT

Understanding God's Mission

To be able to participate in and support a plan, you must understand the mission. God was absolutely clear on the mission to bring man to eternal life and permanent communion with Him in heaven. What a big picture! The spiritual world baffles us and we find it easier to ignore than to comprehend, but we must in order to be able to understand this mission.

God's plan for communion with us is challenged every way possible by the opposing spiritual forces of Satan. Working with opposition makes it much harder for a plan to work. We know the outcome. God in heaven will overcome. We want to be on the winning team. To help us in knowing the Father, God gave us some important tools. The biblical accounts are examples of those gone before us that were helpers in God's plan. Jesus' walk on earth made it possible for us to see, learn, and experience the power that God renders to those who claim Him. And the Holy Spirit, who now operates inside us, gives us continual resources to support the Master's plan. Everything we are asked to do from our Master relates to His clearly defined mission. It is the communication that seems to baffle us the most. Many of us would say, "I would do whatever He tells me, if I just knew what that is." God desires to reveal himself to us more than we can ever imagine. There are several reasons why we find it difficult.

Reasons Communication with God May Be Difficult

Negative influences make it hard for us to hear. It seems that there are hundreds of distractions to communion with the Lord. We are hindered by our lack of faith that He can and will speak to us. Until we accept that He can communicate with and direct us, we are not able to get our plans. And when we are too connected to our own desires rather than His, we can't be very useful in our role in the master plan. Each day, we pass by moments when we could connect and respond to requests from above. Because we are human, we will miss some for sure. But life becomes so much more abundant when we surrender to the level that He had in mind. When we begin to realize that we can bring the Lord into our thoughts without lots of formality, we find it much easier to reach Him.

Understanding God's Will for Our Journey

Understanding God's will and our will makes for an important concept in knowing when to act and when to wait. We are on a journey. Proverbs 16:9 ESV says, "In his heart a man plans his course, but the Lord determines his steps." God places in us a desire for what He intends for us to do. Incredibly, we are preprogrammed to become what fits into His master plan. Nursing, engineering, and painting can all be professions that bring rewards. God cares not only about the destination, but also just as much about the steps along the journey.

If we were to really surrender control of the decision making, it would initially feel like traveling down a river in a boat with no oars. We would not be comfortable

Thought of the Week:
God was absolutely clear on the mission: He intended to bring man to an eternal life and permanent communion with Him in heaven.

in that situation. We would immediately start negotiating control of an oar. We might even promise not to actually use the oar, but would like to have it so we could be more at peace while we floated down the river. If I felt called to go to Washington DC from Charlotte, North Carolina, there are many ways I could travel. God is interested in having the right to direct that travel. Why? God has planned many smaller miracles along the way that tie to His master plan. The more I seek His plan for each step, the better my journey goes, the more useful I can be to the Lord, and the more amazed I am at the perfection of His timing.

Don't Double Dribble!

The longer I wait for His plan, the better I do at finding it. Once, in a time of prayer, I came to understand, "Don't Double Dribble." I laughed. The Lord was asking me not to take a step without bouncing it off Him first. How clear that seems in concept. We are taking steps and not even realizing that He might have input, a better plan, or a step that fits more perfectly than our minds have considered.

I came to understand "Don't Double Dribble"…
The Lord was asking me not to take a step without bouncing it off Him first.

Waiting on the Lord is unnatural. A friend of mine who greatly loves the Lord once had a symbolic dream to help her understand why she was not finding success in her career. The dream brought her much clarity. In the dream, she saw herself pulling a cart. The cart was from olden days, with large wheels and a wooden frame. She woke to understand that she was putting the cart before the horse. She was trying to lead instead of following her Master whom she loved. When others say "God is my co-pilot," I say, "I am just His crew."

God, the "Problem Solver"

I have come to a greater understanding now about just how patient we can really be if we want to see God handle the matter for us and deliver a small miracle. In Psalms, David described God as sovereign. I love that adjective because it means "to solve." What is really beautiful about waiting on the Lord is that you find yourself reacting more than acting. Usually, He brings the solution right into my hands. What I am doing looks effortless as it is solved. Recently, when I needed someone to fill a job vacancy, I sought the Lord's direction. I got "nothing." I had to wait and do the work myself, in addition to my normal workload. Weeks passed and my staff was worried. Then, I felt divinely led to put a small ad on the bulletin board at the YMCA where I exercise. Within one hour, Norma called to inquire about the job. No other callers responded. Norma and I thought we should meet to discuss options. At lunch, we shared how amazing it was for both of us that we were connected. Norma relayed she had never once looked at that bulletin board before that day and I had never ever advertised that way.

Norma and I found our fit and she has served in a support role in the creation of this workbook. It took more time to fill the vacancy, but when God brings in the right person for the right job, she is perfect and worth the wait.

God Wants Us to Wait on Him

Why does God want us to wait on Him? He loves to deliver. He loves to please us and meet our needs. He loves to see His plan for us come together for its fit into His master plan. It was miracles that turned the heads of the early followers of Jesus. Our small miracle turns heads today. The more attention we can bring to Him, the closer He is to His divine master plan.

We are often caught not knowing when to plan and when to act. Our schedules are booked. We are busy people. Our time is planned in our day timers, reflecting our priorities. Personally, my favorite days at work are ones where my calendar is open, clear, and available. I like to solve problems and be free to deal with whatever comes up. Few days go as we plan, anyway, and so often the most interesting things happen in what appear to be unplanned situations.

We have all had the experience of wanting to schedule someone important for a vital meeting. We begin the scheduling process by trying to determine when or if that person is available. God works just that way. All He really needs to know is if we are available. While God is interested in the big picture of seeing us arrive at His destination, He is just as interested in the journey He has preordained and scheduled many divine appointments along the way. How does that really work? We need to make time for God. Our schedules become much more interesting when we start our day by surrendering our task list to God's perfect plan for that day. While we are entitled to think, work, plan, and envision our path, the vital element for a divine appointment is to step away from the plans emotionally, remaining detached enough to go with the flow. What flow? The flowing of events around us, which evolve rather than being completed under our control. God is the scheduler. He is searching our hearts and minds daily to know just how available we are for Him. Will we give Him control of our schedule? A little, a lot, or completely?

God is the scheduler. He is searching us daily to know just how available we are. Would you give Him control of your schedule? A little, a lot, or completely?

Waiting Takes Incredible Faith

Recently, our friend Dan invited Brian and I to the Big Twelve college conference championship football game in his hometown. It would involve making flight and travel arrangements in advance for us to attend. Brian encouraged me to go since I love sporting events. We both thought that the invitation was a nice offer and a God-supported plan. Dan was to handle obtaining tickets for what was sure to be a "sold-out game." I would make my travel plans. An hour before the game, Dan said to me, "Trust me on the tickets." As we approached the stadium from the parking lot, it became clear to me that Dan had not yet purchased tickets for this sold-out game. Dan said, "Just watch as God directs this. It will be much more of a memory by waiting on God for His plan." As we were walking up to the gate, the game had already started. Tickets were sold out at the box office. The scalpers had left the area, having sold all their offerings, too. From nowhere, a man in a dark trench coat walked up and asked, "You guys need tickets?" Yes! With the game already started, the tickets were marked down to half price. Upon entering the stadium, there were no crowds to work through, no lines at the concession stands, and we had only missed four minutes of actual playtime. The seats were club-level premium choice with a great view and first-class patrons surrounding them. I was stunned at the trust, guts, and remarkable outcome in obtaining these tickets. Dan said, "See what God can do when you trust Him for it?" When I told Brian the story, he was shocked and impressed with Dan's faith.

Few of us would be comfortable waiting to this extreme of an unscheduled plan. From this trip, I saw a new summary of faith: the longer you wait, the bigger the miracle. Allowing God to make the miraculous small appointments with which His desire to impress you can only be accomplished when we realize that He is the scheduler. Dan gave God control and put it to the test for God to oversee the details of the appointment. What Dan didn't know is that his faith would inspire another

Trust in the Lord with all thine heart; and lean not unto thine own understanding.
—Proverbs 3:5

level of understanding for me to see what God really wants from us when He says, "Trust in the Lord with all thine heart; and lean not unto thine own understanding" (Prov. 3:5).

If God wanted our faith to stop at the acceptance of Jesus as our Savior, He would not have promised to direct our path too. "Thy word is a lamp unto my feet, and a light unto my path" (Ps. 119:105). Freeing ourselves to be someone's divine appointment for the day fits into the bigger picture as those small miracles turn thoughts and minds to Him. Those with a beginner's faith may pause to say, "God, You must be real." It was miracles that turned the heads of the early believers. The same results can be found today through divine appointments.

God is ready to amaze you and those around you as you pass your calendar to Him. Watch what He will do for you when you invite Him to plan your days by praying more and striving less, waiting until you receive confirmation to act, and letting Him map the journey.

Without Christ, the Wages for Our Sin Are Death

One thing you can count on is that God never moves from His mission. He intends to save the world one person at a time, using those who will cooperate with Him to share His plan of eternal life. Sin cannot be part of His plan. While we were sinners, He saved us in order to forgive us and remove us from that sin. Growing up, I just could not get it. Why did Jesus have to die on a cross? Why would the Bible say the wages of sin are death? What made it so Jesus had to die? I learned that this has to do with a plan to overcome sin on earth and give us a chance at eternal life, as explained by Charles Stanley in a sermon entitled "His Precious Blood." In essence, Stanley made the most logical explanations I've ever heard in the following points.

As parents to our children, it is our job to punish deviance and reward good behavior. It's often a tough call—to show love and yet stop the incorrect actions of our children. Parents must discipline their children. My own earthly father gave my mother the highest of all compliments. He said what she had done right was to take the time to teach right and wrong in even the smallest of matters. God the Father must work with much the same principle.

He is the judge and jury for Earth. If criminals keep sinning with no consequences, the world would become unfit. If each criminal, no matter what he or she did, was sentenced to die for his or her crime, we would claim the judge ruthless and uncaring. Only a few people would be allowed to live. For the most part, judges today are respected and honored for their role in upholding the law of the land. Without them, the world's corruption would grow.

God, who created the world, had a dilemma. He would ultimately solve this through Jesus. Before Jesus, the sacrificial act of atonement for sin was in the slaying of an animal. One wonders how entire breeds of sheep survived to this day, considering all the sacrifices it would have taken to attempt to cleanse the world; but this was only a temporary measure until Jesus could come and prepare a way for our salvation.

Without Christ, the wages for our sin are death. We were supposed to be on that cross between the two criminals, yet Jesus went in our place. He paid the price so we might avoid our own criminal charges. It was God who showed mercy on us.

He could not ignore the sins of this world, nor could He be merciless and sentence us to die for any sin.

Without Jesus stepping in to take our place or rescue us, our death would result in eternal separation from God. God's plan for us was companionship with Him eternally in heaven. He placed us on this journey. God is ruler of the universe. At the end of time, Jesus will become the ruler of the earth. Until then, Satan will continue to be the prince of the earth until Jesus' complete and final victory is won. Isaiah 45:23 says, "Every knee will bow down to Him." All persons will praise Him. Jesus fully understood why He was standing in our place when even His own mother and His disciples could not completely comprehend. He died beside criminals. This was symbolic of how far He would go to pay for our crimes, to free us from our debt to God.

Every knee will bow down to Him.
—Isaiah 45:23

Normally, we expect to see each criminal repay his or her own debt to society. We take a life for a life. Without Jesus' death on the cross, the devil ruled the Earth. There was no door to heaven until Jesus' victory on the cross. He started the process for us of life after death by opening heaven's gate. When someone saves another human being's life, that person may say, "I owe them my life." To Jesus we say, "Yes!" It was the blood that came out of Jesus' body that confirmed the deal was done. Jesus is the Lamb who died and set us free from our own obligation to die. God knew from the very beginning this would be His plan. God was said to have literally walked in the Garden of Eden by Adam's account: "And they heard the voice of the Lord God walking in the garden in the cool of the day: and Adam and his wife hid themselves from the presence of the Lord God amongst the trees of the garden" (Gen. 3:8 ESV). It was Adam's sin that started the plan for our salvation rolling.

Blood was and is one of the few parts of man for which medical science has not found a true substitute. The function for blood in our veins is to carry oxygen, the breath of our life. Jesus' blood was royal. It came from God the Father through the Virgin Mary.

When my own son, Scott, was born without the blood volume to sustain him, I immediately began to marvel at the complexity of blood—oxygen carrying, energy building. It holds the immune system, the blood clotting platelets, and cleansing systems. Scott had blood with few red blood cells. His blood was weak, not rich.

Jesus' blood is rich. His blood was rich enough and regal enough to suffice for the debt of trillions. Man's blood is his cleansing system, which is symbolic of how Jesus' blood will spare us and cleanse us. The blood runs through every inch of our body, from head to toe, through miles and miles of veins, capillaries, and arteries. His unselfish agony brought us eternal freedom. He was a man. He had a choice to accept this assignment. His burden for this task was mammoth. It was so great that He would sweat drops of blood, symbolic of the substance that would set us free from the penalty of sin, which is death.

Jesus' blood is rich. His blood was rich enough and regal enough to suffice for the debt of trillions.

There Is No Greater Sacrifice

People who have faced the loss of a child can truly understand what it meant for Father God to send His son to the cross. Though Scott is as healthy as he can be now, I came close to seeing the pain of the death of a child. There is no greater sacrifice. It was from Scott's birth crisis that I came to understand why Jesus had to die on the cross as prophesied in Isaiah 19:20, "That the Lord would send a great one, a Savior." It was because criminals in those days were put to death on a cross, because people sacrificed pure animals to atone for individual sins, and because there was nothing greater for God to sacrifice for all humanity than His son. Jesus' blood was the only thing in the entire universe valuable enough to clear the record for all sinners. God, who rules with truth and grace, had to respond to sin rather than ignore it.

By accepting Jesus as the Savior of the world, we have accepted the remarkable gift of our place in eternity. It is by this faith we are spared. So how are we spared? John 3:16 says it is by belief in the Lord Jesus Christ: "For God so loved the world, that He gave His only begotten Son, that whosoever believeth in Him should not perish but have everlasting life" (John 3:16). While almost all religions evolve around the concept of Godhead, it is the belief in Jesus that promises us life in heaven after death. The concept is that simple: Jesus.

While the Jews are still waiting for their Savior, we accept Jesus as this person—not Buddha or Mohammed or Rapha, and not by our works or deeds or act of baptism. It is only through faith in Jesus that we are saved. Romans 10:13 states, "For whosoever shall call upon the name of the Lord shall be saved."

What Must You Do to Be Saved?
Most Christian faiths see the plan of salvation as a three-step process—repent, believe, and confirm.

1. Repent means we are remorseful for both past and future sins. The questions presented are:
    A. Do you believe you have sinned, and are you sorry for this?
    B. Do you truly desire to strive for less sin in the future?

2. Believe in Jesus!
    A. Do you believe He died on the cross and was resurrected to give you life after death?
    B. Are you willing to give yourself to Jesus to be useful?

3. Confirm your decision by acceptance within your own heart.
    A. Do you accept yourself as now saved?
    B. Will you confess Jesus before all men, be baptized, and serve within your church?

Must we be baptized to go to heaven? Not according to the Bible. It is by simple faith in Jesus we are saved.

Does unforgiven sin keep us from heaven? Not according to the Bible. All sins are equal; none are greater or worse. It is not through forgiveness but belief in Jesus we are saved. According to this, even suicide will not hold us out of heaven.

Can we confirm the salvation of others? So often we want to think this job belongs to pastors, clergy, and ordained laymen, but that is not what Jesus said. He commissions us to go into the world and share this news. This is the "service" part of our commitment, yet few regular churchgoers take this role seriously.

Why do we believe in baptism? Because Jesus was baptized as an example; this is symbolic of the new life. The born-again life that God desires for us is life that truly looks to sin less and serve more. The Lord Jesus told us in Matthew 10:32,

For God so loved the world, that He gave His only begotten Son, that whosoever believeth in Him should not perish but have everlasting life"
—John 3:16

What Must You Do to Be Saved?
1. *Repent!*
2. *Believe in Jesus!*
3. *Accept salvation!*

"Whosoever shall confess me before men, him will I confess before my Father which is in Heaven."

The Bible is clear that we are saved by faith, not by deeds.

"For by grace are ye saved through faith, and that not of yourselves; it is the gift of God. Not of works, lest any man should boast," says (Eph. 2:8–9).

The plan was that each believer should yield to the prompting of the Holy Spirit and share his or her faith with others in a multiplying effect. Jesus commissioned twelve disciples. He alone as a single pastor could not do it all.

Minimum vs. Maximum

The minimum plan of salvation is to accept Jesus as the Savior of the world. The maximum plan is to work to take others to heaven with you.

In the movie *Schindler's List*, Schindler demonstrated the burden one should feel for the saving of the souls of others. While he had given up all his earthly riches to buy the lives of thousands of Jews from execution, he in his own heart felt the burden for the lives he did not save. Near the close of the movie, there was a very dramatic scene as Schindler realized that he could have saved more Jews if he had only tried. This was what Christ had in mind for us, that we would carry the burdens of the souls that cross our path. Yet, time and time again, we ignore the call. When we finally surrender in completeness to the Holy Spirit, the Schindler-type burden overcomes us to do more, love more, and accept the responsibility for the sharing of salvation with our fellow man. If we had the cure for cancer to save the lives of others and did not share it, we would be considered heartless and be condemned by our fellow man. Yet, we have the secret for eternal life, and we choose to hold the secret in silence.

When baptized, we believe we receive the baptism of the Holy Spirit. This is a symbolic act. The Holy Spirit, however, is actually received when we, in ourselves, accept Jesus. From there, the growth process is based on our level of commitment. The choice is ours to go for the minimum or the maximum plan. The greater our commitment to serve, the greater the flowing of the fruits of the Holy Spirit. These fruits, defined in Galatians 5:22–26, are love, joy, peace, patience, kindness, goodness, faithfulness, meekness, and self-control. These are character-shaping traits that make us more Christlike. The Holy Spirit teams with our conscience. Our conscience is heightened as we submit to Christ. The Holy Spirit uses our conscience as the means to talk to us, advise us, and guide us onto the right paths.

To receive the gifts of the Holy Spirit, it requires a commitment to the maximum plan. *These gifts include knowledge, wisdom, discernment of others, prophecy, tongues, interpretation of tongues, faith, healing, and miracles* (see 1 Cor. 12:8–11). The more the fruits of the Holy Spirit shape our character, the better equipped we become to allow these gifts to grow in us. These are the power-working, action-oriented vehicles of our Christian walk.

As always, with Christ, the choice is ours to accept the minimum service role, accounting for only your own soul, or the maximum service, by accepting accountability for the souls of those who cross your path. To know when to reach out to serve, we need to be in communication with the Holy Spirit. It is through experiencing God's voice today that we accept our service in Christ's plan to save the entire world.

For by grace are ye saved through faith, and that not of yourselves; it is the gift of God. Not of works, lest any man should boast.
—Ephesians 2:8–9

... the fruits of the Holy Spirit. These fruits, defined in Galatians 5:22–26, are love, joy, peace, patience, kindness, goodness, faithfulness, meekness, and self-control.

The gifts of the Holy Spirit ... include knowledge, wisdom, discernment of others, prophecy, tongues, interpretation of tongues, faith, healing, and miracles.
—1 Corinthians 12:8–11

REVIEW & INTROSPECTION

CHAPTER 1: THE MISSION STATEMENT

WEEK 1

1. What are some of the obstacles that prevent us from communicating with God?
   Which do you believe hinders you the most?

   _____

   _____

2. Recall a time in your past when you "double dribbled" and suffered the consequences of it. Explain.

   _____

   _____

3. Now recall a time in your past when you heard God's voice and acted on it.
   What were the results?

   _____

   _____

4. Double dribbling can cause you to step outside of God's will for your life. Say this short prayer to prevent that from happening:

   Lord, forgive me for taking steps without bouncing them off of You first. Help me to consult with You before every move I make. Teach me to hear You clearly when You speak to me. Help me to stay within the boundaries of Your will for my life. In Jesus' name I pray, amen.

5. My friend Dan waited an hour before a "sold-out game" to get tickets because he had radical faith in God. On a scale of one to ten, what is your level of faith? (You can be honest here. The goal is for us to grow, and I am only here to help you!)

   a. If your level is lower on the scale, what are some ways to increase your faith?
   b. If your level is on the high end of the scale, what are some ways for you to take your level of faith in God even higher?

6. Accepting the maximum plan of salvation means you commit to taking others to heaven with you. In the _margin to the left,_ list the names of your unsaved friends and family members. Now, ask the Holy Spirit how you can "serve" them and show the love of Christ to them. Write your responses next to each name. _Make plans to "serve" them this week._

Scripture References: *What do these Scriptures mean to you personally?*

Proverbs 3:5

_____

Psalm 119:105

_____

Matthew 10:32

_____

Galatians 5:22–26

_____

MAKING IT LOOK APPEALING

Let Your Light Shine

Somehow we have gotten the view of Christianity backwards. We are supposed to make it look appealing. By allowing God to make good on all the promises in the Bible, we are supposed to draw the world's interest to Him. When we just focus on the rules of the faith, rather than the promises and the power made available to us, we confuse the nonbeliever. Mathew 5:16 ESV says, "In the same way, let your light shine before men, that they may see your good deeds and praise your Father in heaven."

Some years ago, I received an invitation to bring a message to a chapel on the U. S. navy base in Sasebo, Japan. The attendees were to be sailors, their families, and navy base personnel. In a time of expectant prayer, I asked the Lord to show me how to bring these young men to understand what He wants from us. *I came to understand that God called us to be fishers of men, not hunters of men.* He was deliberate with His description. God really intended that the art of bringing men to Him should be a passive approach. We are to stand there and make it look appealing, just like the bait on a hook. And when we have drawn their interest with our peacefulness, our successfulness, and our virtues, we will find ourselves standing on the moment of opportunity to credit the source, to glorifying God.

Become a Manager, Not a Hoarder

God intended to establish us in our field and to allow us to rise to places of recognition, because in that, His power becomes clearer to those who have only known an invisible God. The more attention I get, the more influence I have. God may own the cattle on a thousand hills and be the controller of the world, but He is counting on me to gain position to render myself and my resources to His use. Mother Teresa lived like God's best example. In her mission to feed the hungry and care for sick children in poverty-stricken lands, she managed thousands of dollars of funds. We are told that upon her death, she could put her own possessions in a shoe box. By raising her stature among man, she commanded greater responsibilities and resources, which she in turn gave back to His work. She was a manager of resources, not a user or hoarder. In the book of Luke, Jesus told a parable of the servant who was faithful with a little. The master of the faithful servant increased his riches and responsibility to be over ten cities. Greater responsibility is given when we have been proven responsible with little. It is not about the personal riches. It is about managing our resources for the Lord. Only then can He trust us enough to take us to the place of higher status He has chosen for us. God moves slowly in testing most of us on our ability to handle more status. Why? Because part of the test is in discovering if we can love Him through the droughts, the emptiness, the unknown, and the nonsupport of others. When you're waiting, enjoy knowing that God is watching. The stronger you can hold out for Him, the higher He can take you.

WEEK

2

Thought of the Week:
By earning worldly credibility, we find moments to share the greater source of our power, abilities, and success. God is glorified. Man is amazed.

He Cares about the "Small Stuff"

Life is about control so much of the time. We think we are happy when we have control. God is really ready to take that position for us. He is asking all the time, "How much control are you going to give me?" Some years ago, the saying came out, "Don't sweat the small stuff." The punch line is, "Everything is the small stuff." God intended to handle the small stuff. So why is it that we just trust Him for the big stuff?

Maybe we just haven't accepted how much He desires to reveal Himself to us. The more I cast the task upon Him, the more I can see that He cares beyond my limited thinking about even the smallest details of my life. As adults, the pressures we carry can be large. We worry ourselves with job security, mortgage payments, teenagers' decision-making, and acceptance by our fellow man. We long for the carefree life of childhood, when someone else took care of all our concerns.

Bingo! God intends to take care of all of our concerns. He made that clear in His infinite promises in the Bible. We of little faith try to carry our concerns, as if God is too busy to handle more than our big requests. The miraculous finding is that God desires to reveal Himself to us more than we can ever imagine. The life described in the Bible sounds carefree leaning on an omnipotent God to deal with everything for us.

We are control freaks! God is a gentleman in His posture. He neither takes our demands nor manipulates us. He waits for us to come to the wisdom of the Bible. He longs to know us, to reveal Himself, and to stir the world around us into His perfect plan for us. Only through our cooperation can He be our solution. First Corinthians 13:11 NLT says, "When I was a child, I talked like a child, reasoned like a child." For most of us, God is still waiting for us to mature to think, speak, and act like an adult, mature in our knowledge of what He desires to do for us.

Have you ever been standing in a moment in time when you knew that you were exactly where God wanted you to be for that instant? A place where you knew beyond a shadow of a doubt that His plan for you was upon you? If so, then you remember the absolute euphoria, comfort, and feeling of success that the Lord intended for His people to have when they walk with Him. Few have taken Him up on the promises alluded to in 1 Corinthians 2:9 NLT, "No eyes have seen, no ears have heard … the things I have for you." We limit the plan by not believing Him for the bigger plan He envisions for us. As I share the workings of a career path God built for me, I hope to convey how serious He is about taking each of us to the perfect plan He has for us.

His Perfect Plan for Me

In April of 1998, I was seated on a trolley bus in Columbia, South Carolina on a beautiful spring night, with fellow members of the South Carolina Governors School. The lights of the city were in front of me and the fellowship warm around me as I felt the world stop in my soul for a moment frozen in time. For months, I had known that God was calling me to a new place in my career. Having served for fourteen years as executive director of a non-profit medical rehabilitation center, God was calling me to a new place. I didn't know all the details, but I did believe that He would show me my new work. In a moment that felt like God's presence was upon me, I prayed, "Lord, let me move to a big city, let me build a big company, and let me give You a lot of money." It took. I felt the connection of heaven and

God intends to take care of all our concerns. He made that clear in His infinite promises in the Bible.

earth unlike any prayer I had transmitted in my mind. From my spirit's reaction, I felt that my prayer was consistent with God's perfect plan for me.

For months, I had believed I was to resign and begin a training network for medical rehab personnel. It would be a big leap of faith to leave the $7 million operation behind and start a company in my front bedroom office. People would not understand and would doubt my reasons for leaving. My husband's job was not secure at the government-funded plant where he was employed. I asked the Lord for many signs and directions that this new career path was His perfect plan and place for me. At every turn, I heard yes. I resigned and began to watch the fallout around me, though I never lost the confidence in my belief that a training company for medical rehabilitation professionals would work. As I waited and watched, I was able to walk out, leaving the rehabilitation center as God directed my steps.

It would have been easier for me to resign and exit, but I understood I was to stay to complete every single task, leaving all in order. I was also to work out the pressure and stresses of the change in front of the staff, who were watching to see how I handled the demotion of power and authority. God gave me the grace to do so without regrets. Each time I asked God for confirmation of my future, He would send it.

Martha, a Pentecostal praying woman, became my encourager during those last days at the medical center. She approached me to say, "I don't know how and I don't know why, but I saw you on a trolley bus." *Wow!* She could not have known my prayer. I never mentioned it to anyone. God's presence around me heightened as I moved into my new work with many unknowns. Now seven years later, in Charlotte, North Carolina, and with many hundreds of God-directed steps, my company, Motivations, Inc., is an accredited continuing education company for medical rehab personnel, training more than three thousand therapists annually, generating $1.2 million in gross annual revenue, and bringing knowledge of medical healing for disabled children and adults to more than thirty states in the United States. God is faithful.

Learning to Listen and Act Is an Art

The more I walk under God's perfect plan, the more people are amazed at the results. Doors of curiosity open, and chances arrive each day to calmly and cleverly give God the glory. The greatest earthly resource I have uncovered is in the Holy Spirit's power to me. My average IQ and my modest earthly finances would not alone have carried me. By being able to access the mind of Christ through the Holy Spirit, God guided me. My dear mother's prayer for me in this venture from day one was, "Lord, don't let her get ahead of You." Well said, Mother, and well received by heaven, as it was necessary to keep me on track.

We are often baffled in knowing how much we should use our own earthly talents in balance with God's actions. Should I plan my work if God is going to direct? I have learned to think of planning this way: If I still had only the career, skills and abilities I had when I entered the work force twenty-five years ago, I would not be as useful to Him. The more advanced my knowledge, skills, talents, and resources, the more abilities I have to use under His wise control. The more I use my mind to think ahead, vision, ponder, consider, plan, and prepare, the more ready I am to act when He shows me where I am going. Am I wasting myself to work through things in my mind when I really am going to wait on Him? By

Now seven years later ... with many hundreds of steps directed by God, my company generates $1.2 million in gross annual revenue and brings knowledge of medical healing for disabled children and adults to more than thirty states in the United States. God is faithful.

working through my thoughts, options, and plans, I am more ready to respond as God directs.

For example, in preparing to go to the U. S. navy base to speak, my friends were praying that one of the huge ships would be docked that weekend. When all the ships are out to sea, the base is very quiet. Only in God's perfect plan could it have happened that my trip corresponded with the arrival of the U. S. secretary of the navy, which brought all five major ships to the base that weekend. The chapel was packed, providing me the chance to share far beyond any plans I could have been responsible for making. How did I find that weekend? By letting God pick the weekend from a series of options through prayer time. I surrendered to offer any input on that date. My freedom of control on this matter paved the way.

What I do know is that when I find and follow the Master's plan, in His perfect timing, the world around me notices. It is a more perfect plan, with a more awesome outcome.

Learning to listen and act is an art. This book looks at the process for growing those skills. What I do know is that when I find and follow the Master's plan, in His perfect timing, the world around me notices. It is a more perfect plan, with a more awesome outcome. There will be amazing details to the plan that are so perfect they can't be explained.

God intended to make our faith in Him look appealing, as one of the basic ways to draw men unto Him. In John 12:32 ESV we are told, "But I, when I am lifted up from the earth, will draw all men to myself." By earning worldly credibility, we find moments to share the greater source of our power, abilities, and success. God is glorified. Man is amazed.

REVIEW & INTROSPECTION

CHAPTER 2: MAKING IT LOOK APPEALING

1. There is a distinct difference between being "fishers of men" and being "hunters of men." In your own words, describe the difference.

   _____

   _____

2. Take a quick inventory of your life. Are you handling God's resources well, like Mother Teresa or the faithful servant in the Parable of the Talents? Why or why not?

   _____

   _____

3. *We are control freaks.* God wants to take care of all our concerns, but oftentimes we don't let Him. In your opinion, why don't we relinquish control to Him?

   _____

   _____

4. Have you ever experienced a dream, vision, or divine experience, like I had on the trolley bus, which was later confirmed to you by someone with whom you had not shared it? Explain.

   _____

   _____

5. In what ways do you bring glory to God daily—in your work, home, church, or community—so that men may see and be amazed?

   _____

   _____

Scripture References: *What do these Scriptures mean to you personally?*
Matthew 5:16

_____

Luke 19:11–27

_____

1 Corinthians 2:9

_____

John 12:32

_____

UNDERSTANDING THE WILL OF GOD

WEEK

3

God's Perfect Will versus His Permissive Will

It is a divine concept that we humans have been given free will to run our lives however we choose. God chose us before we ever chose Him. He wants us to choose Him not by force or coercion but by love. Giving us the freedom to handle our destiny was one of the important concepts of His love.

There have been many discussions through generations on the topic of free will. As Christians, we are told in many ways and places in the Scriptures that God has a plan for each of us. Proverbs 20:24 ESV says, "A man's steps are directed by the Lord. How then can anyone understand his own way?"

During a time of prayer, a friend relayed to me in writing this understanding: God has a perfect will and a permissive will. As good Christians, we can take on many good initiatives under our own creation. We can do kind deeds and good works. We can live morally and properly. We can reach people for Him in helpful ways. A determined spirit can be good but not perfect in doing the actual tasks for which we are called upon. Actions that are under God's permissive will may be good, but it is different than acting in God's perfect will. To follow God's perfect will, we take the time to listen and then hear and then act. Otherwise, we can become confused and our determined, permissive will gets in the way.

Few choose to wait for the opening and direction of God's perfect will. It is in God's perfect will that He is glorified and we live for God and die to self. Self-efforts are deceiving, though they may look and feel wonderful, refreshing, and good. There is no lasting glory for God other than operating a task in His perfect will. It takes a greater wisdom to seek the Master for divine direction. This wisdom lifts up God so that others are drawn in. When God's perfect will is carried out, the work is seen and felt as anointed. Nonbelievers marvel at the results, and believers bask in the glow that they see from the touch of God on the task.

It Is God Who Raises and Anoints

How do you perform God's will on task? You must wait for His direction on the smallest of steps. God gives His glory to those who wait. He will mount up, and as He arises within them, they will know it's Him, for God Himself is the one to rise and to anoint. Waiting on Him brings clarity where there was once confusion. Waiting allows for harmony among the workers. Waiting allows for perfection of the task as God's perfect will flows.

A dear couple was ready to plan their wedding. Completely convinced that God ordained this marriage, they were determined to trust Him for each step. Unlike others planning weddings, they did not act on any single task until directed. As they waited, they were prompted for each task in small, miraculous ways. The cake bakers found them in a parking lot, the invitations were offered by a friend, and the church pastor was asked when God led them. As they prepared for the day, many would have wondered if they covered all the details. They rested in God's direction. People who attended the wedding called it a divinely anointed

Thought of the Week:
To follow God's perfect will, we take the time to listen and then hear and then act.

Completely convinced that God ordained this marriage, they were determined to trust Him for each step. Unlike others planning weddings, they did not act on any single task until directed.

experience. Few could rest and give God control of each detail, but that was how He meant it to be in working with us.

Who Has the Power? Using It to Find God's Will

Call unto me, and I will answer thee, and show thee great and mighty things, which thou knowest not.
—Jeremiah 33:3

What is really amazing is how patient God is with us. His perseverance to allow us to sometimes work under our own permissive will and occasionally find His perfect will is a continual showcase of His abundant, patient love for us. He is hoping we will catch on, that in time we will see the difference and understand how and when we are operating under His perfect direction. His wisdom is explained in Jeremiah 33:3, "Call unto me, and I will answer thee, and show thee great and mighty things, which thou knowest not."

In Matthew 16:15 NLT and 19 Jesus said to His disciples, "Who do you say I am?" Then Jesus explained the power that He would make available to us by saying, "I will give you the keys of the kingdom of heaven, and whatever you bind on earth shall be bound in heaven, and whatever you loose on earth shall be loosed in heaven." With this power, you are stepping into God's will to rein in His will for you. We have been called to obey His Word. David often spoke in the Psalms about how God's Word comforted him. David was fellowshipping with God directly and hearing His word. We can also do this if we move ourselves to His perfect service. In my own life, I came to know and understand God's ways and His will in a most real experience through the birth of my son. Having been led to have a child, my husband Brian and I believed that we were operating in God's perfect will on this matter.

My doctor considered mine to be a perfectly normal, textbook pregnancy. When hearing the baby's heartbeat for the first time, the doctor said it was a very strong heartbeat. This baby was active. I received a rogaime shot as a prevention, since Brian and I had opposite blood types, which can cause the mother's immune system to attack a baby with an opposite blood type. So, from February to August 21, 1989, I prepared myself to receive our baby.

On the evening of Monday, August 21, 1989, I realized something was going wrong. The baby was hurting me. I could not sleep and started having nausea, vomiting, and weakness. In the middle of the night, I called my doctor, which was unlike me. Thanks to the good advice from the night operator, I had her put my doctor on the line. I told him I was confident the baby was sick. At 2:00 am, he said, "How do you know that?"

"I just know," I said.

He planned to see me the first thing the next morning, but by then I was having contractions without dilating. I spent the morning on fetal monitors. A nurse in training said to her mentor in front of me, "There is a strong heartbeat but no fetal movement." After a sonogram to estimate the baby's size and lung development, the doctor made a life-saving decision. He delivered our son by C-section at 2:12 pm, August 22, 1989, and found a baby who was mentally alert but physically limp, with extreme anemia and an enlarged heart.

I had not yet held my baby, but they rushed him past me on a cart. The anesthesiologist said, "Look to your left," and he passed by, I saw his eyes, totally alert and scanning the delivery room, following the sounds and voices. That moment was priceless. Right then I believed, no matter what was wrong, his mind worked.

Within minutes, I was moved to recovery and was advised that our baby weighed five pounds nine ounces. This was good for a baby delivered five weeks before his due date. They needed to transfer him to another hospital to deal with his heart. By then I was moved to my assigned room. The doctor came in to advise us of plans to transport our baby with our permission. Our immediate thoughts were that he would be sent to another state, possibly to New York City or Cincinnati, Ohio. Instead, our baby was going to the Level 1 Neonatal Intensive Care Unit at the Medical Center College of Georgia (MCG), just two blocks away. Heart surgery was a possibility. Once again, my confidence kicked in, and in my mind I said to the doctor, "You can do whatever you need to, but nothing is wrong with his heart." No one knew why his hemoglobin was so low. He had only 20 percent of his red blood volume left. This level would not normally sustain life. Transfusions would be required immediately.

After much company and activity in my hospital room, Brian went to MCG to check in on Scott. No one had any more information to offer. That night as we slept in my hospital room, and we both had the deepest sleep we had had in months. The rest was needed.

The Lord Was with Us

The next day, my progress was steady. We talked by phone to doctors, insurance companies, and hospital nurses, and still no one could tell us why our baby was sick. Yet, something remarkable occurred.

Brian remembered a dream he had during the night of deep sleep. He saw Scott lying in his intensive care bed, and beside him at the end of the bed were two large, adult-sized male angels with their wings folded, standing with their hands on his intensive care bed tray. Their hair was neatly groomed, and their wings complete with intricate feathers, like those of doves. The angels were standing in the exact place the two grandmothers had stood by the baby's bed the day before at Scott's birth. As he recalled this, we were filled with emotion. I knew the Lord was with us. Also, I remembered the Lord had directed us to have a child, so I believed He would never have called us to this if He did not plan to save our baby. The words and direction of the Lord were powerful comfort to us. A Scripture was given to me from Philippians 1:6 NIV: "He who began a good work in you will carry it on to completion."

So, we spent the next two days recalling the dream and vision of the angels. Our prayer was that these angels would stand there and guard our baby while he recovered. Yet, that Thursday was still filled with the mystery of what was wrong with Scott. He was no longer making his own blood in the bone marrow. This discovery sparked all kinds of rare medical speculation, which frightened us.

Thursday night, in the hospital room, knowing I would be going home the following day without my baby, we prayed the deepest prayer of our married life. We prayed that God would give us a sign the next day that Scott was going to be okay, so we could be patient while our baby recovered in the hospital. When we left the hospital Friday morning without our baby, it was, of course, a very low point for me. The sadness hurt so deeply. The Holy Spirit felt my pain, and within minutes the voice of God sounded again, this time in another form.

After passing three drug stores, we finally parked our car in the parking lot of one. I sat in the car, while Brian ran in for the prescriptions I needed. I started

I remembered the Lord had directed us to have a child, so in my mind, He would never have called us to this if He did not plan to save our baby ...

singing songs in an attempt not to become depressed and assure myself that my baby would be okay. And then it happened.

The interpretation of Brian's dream was revealed. My thoughts were filled with an understanding, an understanding that I could not have possibly created. The dream showed angels standing by our baby because he was going to stay on earth. They were not flying over him to take him to heaven. As that thought or revelation consumed me, with excitement and praise, I was covered with chills and totally overcome with emotion. Tears ran down my cheeks.

A young black mother of two little children walked past my car at that very moment. I felt embarrassed that she had seen me crying, but within minutes, she turned around, walked back to my car, and tapped on the window. I rolled down my window, and this beautiful African American lady, whom I did not know and had never seen before, placed her hand on my shoulder and said, "Your baby is going to be okay. It will be fine. You should be happy. This is a happy day. Look at all these flowers around you in the car." She patted my shoulder and said, "It's going to be fine," and walked away. Her act had filled me with God's love. I was touched by her kindness, her perfect timing, and her ability to reach out to me regardless of race.

By the time Brian returned to the car, I was almost hyperventilating. I knew he would think I was saddened, rather than elated. As quickly as I could get it out, I said, "The angels were standing, weren't they? They weren't flying, they were standing?"

He said, "Yes."

I tried to tell him all that had just transpired in the past few moments. The young woman had actually seen him at the door of the drug store with his "It's a boy" badge on and asked him if she could talk to me. The compassion and timing of her words were amazing. God used her voice to carry His voice to me. My thoughts, which had provided me with direction to have this child, were motivated by the Holy Spirit to interpret Brian's dream. The Lord talked to us through Brian's dream. So, even though the puzzling trauma of Scott's sickness was undiagnosed, I had what I needed—God's confirmation of Scott's recovery. That had been our exact prayer, that He would give us a sign so we could be patient with his recovery.

After my return home, I was then able to go see Scott in the intensive care unit for the first time. He was covered with wires, monitors, meters, and personnel. Yet, as he heard my voice, he reacted with obvious excitement by kicking his legs, waving his arms, and blowing bubbles. The staff said, "Look at that. He knows you are his mother." I felt that, too. On the seventh day of his life, I was finally allowed to hold him. He was unwired and placed in my hands. I held him out in front of me with extended arms, looking at his front and back and then kissing the back of his neck. To this day, I tell him that's my spot. Later, as I shared with my friend Allyson about my first kiss to Scott's neck, she said, "I have to tell you this. I don't know how I know this, but I believe that place (on his neck) was meant to be special for Scott, as it is the part of him (his body) that faces the Lord when he bows his head to pray."

Within eight days, Scott's mystery was diagnosed. The rogaime shot had not worked for me, as I have a rare antibody. Only 1 percent of the mothers in this situation have this particular reaction, so it was easily overlooked. My immune system had actually treated this baby as a foreign body, with my antibodies attacking

The Lord talked to us through Brian's dream ... I had what I needed—God's confirmation of Scott's recovery.

his red blood cells one at a time. The obvious catastrophe had been avoided by the doctor's decision to deliver Scott early. Another day and there would have been no red blood cells left to sustain him.

His heart was fine and had actually done its own life-sustaining work by pumping the limited red blood cells through as fast as possible to allow him to survive. I knew it. There was nothing wrong with his heart. It was the doctor's original comment on Scott's strong heartbeat in the womb that was the basis of my belief. And the doctor was correct, figuratively speaking, that Scott's heart was enlarged, as his kindness is often shown to many people he meets.

Scott's bone marrow began to make his blood fast on his actual due date in October. Through the first five weeks of his life, we had Scott's hemoglobin tested almost daily. He was just not physically mature enough to rebuild the lost blood as a premature baby. Knowing that Scott's hemoglobin was a three at birth, the pediatrician phoned me in October 1989. The excitement in his voice made me picture him standing on his desk when he called to say, "It's a twelve!" We were out of the woods and on target with the normal twelve to fifteen!

Prepare for Service

During the time from Scott's birth to fully recovering, I was amazed at the expressions of love, gestures of kindness, and prayer sent up on behalf of our son. Brian and I had led a socially quiet life, and yet all of a sudden, there were several hundred people supporting us—family, friends, employees, neighbors, and even people who never knew us but had heard of our need. It was so touching to be reminded of how caring people can be to each other during times of crisis.

There were many gestures of kindness, all appreciated and all heartfelt. But forever the stranger who comforted me will live in my heart as the perfect example of responding to God's prompting to act in His perfect timing. She could never have known what her actions did to open the spiritual world to me. It is my hope that someday I will be able to find her and share the part of the story that she did not know and how her kindness led to many more rippling effects in God's perfect plans.

God's perfect will is backed by God's perfect love for us. Just like a soldier must train for battle and a teacher must train to educate, so must we prepare ourselves to serve.

But forever the stranger who comforted me will live in my heart as the perfect example of responding to God's prompting to act in His perfect timing. She could never have known what her actions did to open the spiritual world to me.

REVIEW & INTROSPECTION

CHAPTER 3: UNDERSTANDING THE WILL OF GOD

WEEK 3

1. Why has God given us *free will*?

   _____

   _____

2. In your own words, what is the difference between God's *permissive will* and His *perfect will*?

   _____

   _____

3. Who has the power? How can you apply it to a current situation happening in your life to stay within God's will for you?

   _____

   _____

4. While pregnant with my son Scott, I *knew* he was sick. After his birth, I *knew* he would stay here on earth with us. And during his recovery, I *knew* that his heart was healthy and his blood would be normal. God sent me many different assurances throughout the experience. Consider your life. When has God positively affirmed an optimistic outcome to you? How did it make you feel?

   _____

   _____

5. Many people supported us during Scott's birth and his recovery, sharing love, kindness, and prayers. Have you committed to serving others in their time of need? Recount an instance.

   _____

   _____

   * Bonus: Write a short prayer in the margin asking God to communicate His perfect will to you and express to Him your desire to surrender your will to His.

Scripture References: *What do these Scriptures mean to you personally?*
Proverbs 20:24

_____

Philippians 1:6

_____

Jeremiah 33:3

_____

II. PREPARING OURSELVES TO SERVE

Week 4   Christ's Perfect Love 25

Week 5   Gaining Peace 29

Week 6   Building Integrity 39

CHRIST'S PERFECT LOVE

We Have the Ability to Commune with Him

God is love. This basic thought is paramount to how our relationship with the Father works. God desires fellowship with us far more than we could ever desire it for ourselves. It is a divine mystery that we could bring such joy and satisfaction to the Lord who has all of the heavens to enjoy. Created in God's own image and likeness, we have a unique ability to recognize the Father's voice with the capacity for intelligent, satisfying communion with Him. He is far more interested in revealing Himself to us than we are in having Him do so. The Lord desires to bring us into an experience of communion with Him so we might become one with Him in the ongoing purpose of mankind.

The pinnacle of success is when we come to realize that we wish to ask God His counsel and help concerning the needs for which we have a burden. Being asked to marry your future spouse is the position of highest honor; to be chosen. Jesus said, "Ye have not chosen me, but I have chosen you, and ordained you, that ye should go and bring forth fruit, and that your fruit should remain: that whatsoever ye shall ask of the Father in my name, He may give it you" ((John 15:16). In this love relationship, we must come to see the act of obedience as the highest, most beautiful and desired state. It is a relationship where we put our own desires second. God is especially pleased that we accomplish this state of mind. In this state, we are no longer controlled by our desires and actions, but rather, obedience to the Father takes priority. In this we can then overcome temptation and find peace.

Understanding Joyful Surrender

Jesus understood joyful surrender. Jesus lived to do exactly what God the Father wanted Him to, and this is what God desires of us. The goal of the Christian life is never to live well and prosper; it is to live a surrendered life to Christ. He will then fill us with His peace and show us the usefulness to which we have been called. The joy of the surrendered life is in knowing that God always has a tremendous return in mind for our obedience.

The Lord so desires our attention. He is amazingly resilient to let us come back to Him time and time again, no matter how many times we have turned our back on Him. God is of the greatest moral excellence, so absolute in His goodness, so full in His love, that He can expose himself to the agony of rejected love without bitterness or change in His love for us.

His love for us is intimate. He knows us by our thoughts, the number of hairs on our head, and the talents we may not even know we have. He is a God of such great love that we cannot even imagine how close He will let us come to Him. He is of the greatest wisdom—far greater than any counsel we could buy and far more astute in what is going to happen than anyone on earth could know without the companion of the Holy Spirit in us. Father God, Jesus, and the Holy Spirit work hand in hand to supply all of our earthly needs if we can just learn to love obedience. The fact that the Holy Spirit is symbolized by a dove is remarkable

Thought of the Week:
The point of success is when we come to realize that we wish to ask God His counsel and help concerning the needs for which we have a burden.

Father God, Jesus, and the Holy Spirit work hand in hand to supply all of our earthly needs if we can just learn to love obedience.

because a dove is said to have single vision, one focus. God's eyes are on us, and if our eyes are on God, then we are in a place of safety.

Love Conquers All

The Bible has much to say about love. Love conquers all. Love is patient and kind. God is love. We are called to mirror His love. Ephesians 3:17–18 NLT says, "And I pray that you, being rooted and established in love, may have power, together with all the saints, to grasp how wide and long and high and deep is the love of Christ."

He calls for a relationship with us. We determine how deep we want to allow Him into our hearts. Where are we in our faith in Him for handling our life tasks? I have found three levels to help assess your relationship and dependence on Him.

1. **Accepting Child**—You rest in Him, feel peaceful, respond to Him to please Him, and avoid doing wrong to stay at a place of comfort.

2. 2. **Searching Youth**—You talk to Him and expect Him to answer. Obedience feels good even when challenged.

3. **Seasoned Warrior**—You wake each day wanting to know how He will use you. You have relinquished control of the tasks and strive for self-control of your emotions (peacefulness), your body (respect), and your thoughts (honorable).

We Must Learn to Wait

Until our hearts are prepared for Him, we are not ready to serve, to obtain the bigger assignments, or to understand the Holy Spirit in us.

He knows our love by our actions. Joan was a thirty-year-old secretary who had moved back into her parents' home to re-establish her life. While there, she received a phone call asking her to adopt her ten-year-old niece, Trish. No one else in the family could. Joan loved Trish but knew her own situation. Without a moment's hesitation, she responded, "Yes." She knew this was a life-changing phone call. Her love would have to overcome all the challenges of Trish's mental illness and her own employment issues, housing, and finances. With unwavering faith, Joan raised Trish for ten years. As Trish moved on, Joan was saddened. In a time of prayer with Joan, the Lord told me to say, "He loves the innkeeper." In God's eyes, Joan has stepped up when there was no room in the inn. God loved her for that. Joan felt His love in those perfectly timed words from God.

God will convey His love to us, as we need it and when we ask Him to. At a transition point in our lives, Brian and I had looked at lots of new homes and architectural plans. But we were waiting on the Lord to act. My patience was gone. I did not feel I could find God's plan on this subject. Why was He not there? So, I asked a friend to pray with me … for her to pray for God's will into happening. Within one hour, I was a fast food drive-in window and out of the blue words came to mind telling me God saw me as a His sweet lady and the time I had been waiting for was here.

Covered with chills, and in an emotional high, I knew our prayer was heard. God was waiting on me to submit and allow Him to carry out His will. The truth was that Christ had not moved away from me; He was as close as He could be. I

So that Christ may dwell in your hearts through faith. And I pray that you, being rooted and established in love, may have power, together with all the saints, to grasp how wide and long and high and deep is the love of Christ.
—Ephesians 3:17–18

God was waiting on me to submit and allow Him to carry out His will. The truth was that Christ had not moved away from me; He was as close as He could be.

was blocking His presence as I lost patience in waiting, and I needed help to find Him. He was now ready to begin. And more importantly, He comforted me in my waiting to bring the patience needed to not react outside His plan.

Service requires having the heart of a servant. Through all that evolves, He is grooming our heart to be able to wait and act as He so directs.

REVIEW & INTROSPECTION

WEEK 4

CHAPTER 4: CHRIST'S PERFECT LOVE

1. *Jesus lived to do exactly what the Father wanted Him to do.* Knowing this, what do you think is the goal of the Christian life?

   _____

   _____

2. Circle the things that the Lord desires *most* from us.

Love	Sacrifice	Attention
Giving	Obedience	Study
Relationship	Joy	Prayer

3. What are the three levels of relationship with Christ?

   _____

   _____

4. *He loves the innkeeper.* Have you ever responded yes to a call from God that required selflessness? Explain.

   _____

   _____

5. Are you waiting right now for the Lord to move in a particular area of your life? What should you do during your waiting period?

   _____

   _____

*Bonus: *Service requires having the heart of a servant.* Describe a servant's heart in your own words, and then write a short prayer to God in the left margin asking Him to prepare your heart for service.

Scripture References: *What do these Scriptures mean to you personally?*
Ephesians 3:17–18

_____

John 15:16

_____

GAINING PEACE

Peace Is Priceless

Is it truly possible to live stress-free? Could you sell peace if it was advertised? Be the first person on your block to have peace!

The world is searching for relief from our stresses. Expensive counselors and psychiatrists' services are growing in demand. Today, crisis-driven, money-motivated, hectic lifestyles are pressing people to the limit. Yet, the Bible, a collection of the divinely inspired writings of forty men, is full of comments and teachings on how to live without stress.

Peace is priceless. It can't be bought or sold. Individuals can't fake true peace. The disciples had stresses, imprisonment, homelessness, ridicule, and uncertainties about the future. Yet, their accounts of where and how they found peace show us it can be done. Paul, in Philippians 4:11, states, "Now that I speak in respect of 'want': for I have learned in whatsoever state I am, therewith to be content."

Peace is a state of mind, and we control our mind. When we are operating in prayer, we can build positive mental health. It is the Holy Spirit that transcends our own weak spirit to lift us to a point of "contentedness." This peace described in the Bible is defined as a peace that passes all understanding (see Phil. 4:7). It is supernatural and a product only of God. It is not a product that man can create, buy, sell, or teach. Giving up our *wants* is the key, for the more we want, the more demands evolve to propel us past the peace we desire. Mark 8:36 says, *"What shall it profit a man, if he shall gain the whole world and lose his own soul?"*

Remove Stress by Eliminating Sin

There are many robbers of peace: money, power, and physical temptations. These are all forms of sin when taken to the point of prioritizing them above God and therefore, losing peace. It took me years to realize that God gave us His laws, the Ten Commandments, not to make our lives harder but rather to make our lives peaceful. So much of our stress is self-inflicted.

God knew we would not be perfect. In planning to correct our transgressions, the Bible tells us how to remove stress by eliminating sin. We are called to ask for forgiveness. This is not to allow God to slap our hand—certainly not. God's thinking was that we should slap our own hand. God does not take pleasure in watching our remorse for doing wrong. He takes pleasure in watching the cleansing of our conscience through repentance.

Recently in South Carolina, a tragedy unfolded regarding a mother who drowned her two young sons in a lake near the city of Union. While covering up her actions for several days, she was unable to disguise the burden of such a horrible sin. As I followed this story, the most touching revelation was her confession as relayed by law enforcement. This young mother said that due to her confession, she felt the weight of the world lift off her shoulders. It was reported that as she wept in agony, the seasoned investigator wept with her.

WEEK
5

Thought of the Week:
Living the peace is impossible to teach. It is a personal journey of knowing and loving Christ—getting close enough to let Him teach you how it works.

God calls us to confession because secret sins and peace of mind cannot coexist. When we confess our sins, God forgives us before we finish the sentence. In *Psalm 51:10, David asked God to forgive his sin and to create in him a pure heart and renew a right spirit in him.*

In Psalm 51:10, David asked God to forgive his sin and to create in him a pure heart and renew a right spirit in him.

If God Says We Are Forgiven, Then We Are

Forgiving ourselves is often the hardest part of recovering from our past sins. The devil enjoys this one the most because so many of us can't get back to Christ because we can't see that we are forgiven for something He has long since forgiven us for.

How do we forgive ourselves? Through the power of the Holy Spirit. In Philippians 4:13, we are reminded, *"I can do all things through Christ which strengthens me."* In reference to this understanding, I did an extensive search in the Bible for instructions for unforgiveness. I was amazed to find the word "unforgiveness" was never mentioned, not even once. Why would that be? Because if God says we are forgiven, then we are.

There are, however, fifty-five verses in the Bible reminding us to forgive others. How many times should we forgive another? Seventy times seven. It makes sense to think we are also to forgive ourselves as instructed. First John 1:9 says, "If we confess our sins, He is faithful and just to forgive us our sins and to cleanse us from all unrighteousness."

We must initiate this act of asking forgiveness because sin separates us from the Father. David asks the Father to "hide thy face from my sins." Psalm 51:9 Guilt holds us back from peace and we cannot pull close to God. Sin isolates us from God, and if you'll notice, it eventually isolates us from the rest of humanity. And in this lies the most important step in pursuit of peace—closeness to Christ.

Let It All Go!

David described the desire to live in God's presence every day so that He could protect him (see Ps. 27:4). Matthew 6:25 and Luke 12:25 tell us of a logical point of view. If He will take care of the birds, surely we are more important, and can count on Christ. Luke 12:31 reminds us that the Lord will give us all our needs if we make the kingdom of Heaven our first concern. And Jesus Himself declared in a rhetorical question, "When did you need food, and we did not feed you, or clothes, and you did not receive them?" (Matt. 25:37 ESV)

When did you need food, and we did not feed you, or clothes, and you did not receive them?
—Matthew 25:37

The key word in Paul's Philippians 4:11 is the control of our "wants." We are a society obsessed with an unnecessary, undeniable desire for what we want. God cautioned us about the love of money by reminding us it would be harder for a rich man to enter the gates of heaven than for a camel to pass through the eye of a needle. Wow! What a strong image. The love of money leads to greed—a robber of peace—yet we use money for our security rather than Christ's own plan to meet our needs. We feel in control when we have money and seemingly less dependent on Christ.

The same is true of power. As God calls us to humility and wisdom, He becomes our refuge and sword. Christ's leadership calls us to surrender our cross and follow Him. This means submitting our destiny to His hand, not our own. When we cannot release power and be a follower, we cannot pull close enough to let Christ's blanket of peace calm us. The pursuit of power robs peace through the hostility of negative emotions, such as anger, bitterness, vindictiveness, and revenge.

Together, power and money lead to temptation—sin brought on by our own obsessions. Indirect sins can be equally destructive to our inner peace. Worry and fear are pathological forms of unbelief—feeling God is not ready or able to care for us.

Winston Churchill said, "When I look back on all these worries, I remember the story of the old man who said on his deathbed that he had had a lot of trouble in his life, most of which never happened" (*Timeless Wisdoms*, 1995).

God the Father watches our thoughts and just wants us to "give it up!" Stop beating yourself up over "what if's." In Matthew 11:28–30, Jesus said, "Come unto me, all ye that labor and are heavy laden, I will give you rest. Take my yoke upon you and learn of me, for I am meek and lowly in heart; and ye shall find rest unto your sole. For my yoke is easy and my burden is light."

Worry and fear are a pathological forms of unbelief—feeling God is not ready or able to care for us.

Accepting the Gift of Peace

Jesus talked of offering us peace in a very direct sense. The Bible tells us over and over we can find our refuge in Him. As Jesus prepared the disciples for His leaving, He reminded them of the unique peace that would come. In John 14:27 NLT, Jesus says: *"I am leaving you with this gift—peace of mind and heart! And the peace I give isn't fragile like the peace the world gives."*

So, why is it still so hard to get to the point of casting and resting our cares upon Him? The answer is a supernatural gift that defies all logic. Christ, whom we cannot see or touch, promises peace to our stressed-out souls. In order to receive this peace, we must learn to hear God's voice through whatever means that process takes.

Last year, on vacation at the beach with my son, Scott, I met a woman from Michigan named Colleen. As she realized we were both there with kids, she asked if I wanted to go to dinner that evening and talk. I accepted.

During that evening, I found a woman totally overpowered by stresses. She felt guilty about her mother's death because she wished she'd done more to comfort her. She was hurting from the loss of her mother and both grandparents. She was burdened in her marriage. And she was punishing herself for past sins. Her pain was so hard to watch as she talked and cried. I hurt for her. I wanted to show her how to have the peace I've found through Christ, and I tried.

I found myself saying every stress free, peace-giving cliché in the book. "Give it up." "Stop punishing yourself." "Let it go." I had to admit I was getting nowhere at teaching her this concept. But the walls began to fall, and the clouds began to clear when I described my peace—an ability to rest like a baby, energy that was endless, and a mindset that no one could take away my joy. Colleen's belief in Christ was there. She knew and understood what I was saying, but she could not do it. We prayed. We talked, and then we laughed.

The amazing thing about the encounter with Colleen was not what I taught her; it was what she taught me. Living in peace is impossible to teach. It is a personal journey of knowing and loving Christ—getting close enough to let Him teach you how it works. By living in His presence every day, we begin to accept the offer Jesus Christ made to us: to cast all our cares upon Him.

A friend, Caron, shared that she has learned to think of God's ability to take our stresses away by thinking of herself in a boat in the middle of the sea during a storm. As she calls to the Lord to help her, she has come to realize, "Sometimes God calms the sea, and sometimes, instead, He calms me."

It brings Him great pleasure to carry these burdens for us. As my son, Scott, cried one day over being left out of the tag game at recess, I wanted to fix it and stop his hurt. As his parent, I wanted to take Scott's hurt completely away. Jesus feels the same toward us. He is defined in both the Old and New Testaments as the Mighty Counselor. He is the master of all psychiatrists. By relaying our needs to Him in prayer, we can leave the counseling couch lighter.

Josephine, a friend of mine, has the most incredible story of how she obtained peace. A quadriplegic, she was made totally disabled by her husband, who intentionally fired a pistol at her, sending a bullet to her neck at age twenty-six. Josephine was pregnant at the time, and her baby and other children were sent to live with her mother. Now, at age forty-three, she has spent the past seventeen years residing in a nursing home, most of that time confined to a bed.

Today, seventeen years after this incident, I asked her how she had obtained the most radiant peace evident on her face. She said that true peace came to her four years after her accident when she finally completely forgave her ex-husband, who was eventually released from prison for this crime. She thought she had worked through that bitterness, but in a moment of spontaneous emotional healing in the presence of her pastor, she realized that inside she carried anger as if it were a hard black coal. At that moment, in completely releasing her bitterness, God had made Himself more apparent to her than at any other time in her entire life. In her current circumstances, she has found herself completely reliant on Christ.

The Holy Spirit is as real to her as a friend on Earth would be. She has realized that God has taken her out of the rat race and given her time to ponder. In finding her peace on Earth, she believes she has the riches of the Earth. She has realized that she is never alone. She said to me, "God is not fishing, and He has never taken His eyes off me. His ear is always attentive to me; I am never alone." She magnified her commitment to Christ by saying to me, "I can't let anything stand between me and God."

She realizes that Satan would have bet she could never have overcome this adversity to reach total peace. But God knew Josephine. He knew her strength and her faithfulness to love Him through all of life's circumstances. Proof of this peace is in what she said, "I sleep like a baby every night."

Facing Adversity with Joy

The apostles shared over and over their ability to face adversity with joy. Nothing matters but the privilege of serving Jesus. In my own work and life, I have faced challenges with a smile that would seem strange to others. My smile stems from my curiosity to see just exactly how God's going to handle this one.

Recently, driving home one afternoon, my car slowly began to die. I pulled off the road just blocks from my home. This occurred during a period of time when Brian's new business was just starting, and it was obvious God was watching over our finances. I knew immediately God would handle this. I called Brian from my car phone and asked him to meet me. Before he arrived, I sat in the car smiling, curious to see how God would handle this one. Brian gave my car a push and it rolled on its own down the eight blocks home. The next day, after being towed to the dealership, the mechanic said that the fuel pump had to be replaced and would be covered under a factory recall agreement. There was no charge for the service. In two days, I was to be on the road to Atlanta without Brian's ready assistance. It was fun for weeks to tell people of the pleasure in watching God handle this for me.

Herb Cohen, the author of *You Can Negotiate Anything*, uses the words "I care—but not that much," to express his ability to score big on major negotiations. It seems that surrendering our wants allows for the best results.

Sometimes It's Just Life's Misfortunes

Some robbers of our peace have nothing to do with sin; they are just life's misfortunes. In these challenges, we must learn to see the Father as a leader who sees all sides of the issue. From our limited vantage point, we can only see the present stress, pain, and burden. Christ can see the big picture—the growth of character, relationship building with Him, and opportunities to share with others from our pain. In these instances, I have learned to believe that sometimes it is our job to weather the storm—not just feel the rain but walk through it.

From our limited vantage point, we can only see the present stress, pain, and burden. Christ can see the big picture …

A prisoner of war returning from the Vietnam War said he saved his peace through the worst of adversities by the realization that no matter what they took from him—freedom, food, or comfort—they could not take his soul. He was able to sustain his own peace by the knowledge that he still had control of his thoughts and soul.

The disciples showed us, even in facing death in prison, they could keep their peace. Paul said, "To live is an opportunity to serve Christ, yet in dying, well, that was better yet" (Philippians 1:21 TLB). Amazing inner peace is shown in this verse. Only a person totally dedicated to Christ could have even thought of these words. In these situations, Christ has made us a promise. He guaranteed us we would not be given more burdens than we can take (Matt. 11:28). While some seem to resort to pity and hostility, others use these challenges to press closer to Christ. Guess who walks the easier, more honorable path?

In my early days as an executive director, at age twenty-four, operating a financially challenged nonprofit agency, I thought, "Hit me again, I can take it." That mental toughness helped me focus on the job instead of surrendering. Yet, it was Christ in *me* who carried me toward the resolution each time. Peace came as I passed along issues, needs, and stresses with the simple word, "Help."

Peace came as I passed along issues, needs, and stresses with the simple word, "Help."

Why Live a Peaceful Life?

Why would Christ have us at peace? Because life becomes a pleasure when we can see joys of the Earth. When we are under stress, we cannot stop and smell the roses. A friend of mine, Mike, tells of his battle with kidney cancer. After going through medical intervention, a hospitalization was required. The procedure was successful, and God's hand was clearly on Mike's shoulder. When he was released from the hospital, he drove away a new man. During that drive, he experienced the love of life only a man who has faced life's end can appreciate. The flowers were more radiant, the sky bluer, and the air lighter. His burden was lifted, and the world's colors were no longer just bright; they were fluorescent that day.

Burdens blind our vision from God's blessings. We cannot see the gifts He sends—the new experiences and the pleasures of a simple day. Working in medical rehabilitation, I am daily made aware of all the joys we take for granted, such as walking without pain, hearing clearly, and having healthy children. As a medical social worker, it was evident to me that attitudes about recovery directly impact an individual's eventual health.

The more I see the traumas others must live with, the more I have noticed that those with the ability to see good in all things are free to look beyond themselves to others. The second reason God desires us to have peace is that unless we have it ourselves, we cannot reach out to meet others' needs. Maslow, a great psychologist, developed the hierarchy of needs that shows our basic needs are food, water, and clothing. So much of what we want has to do with matters beyond that. I have learned it is unselfish to ask God to meet my own needs so I will be free to ask for the needs of others. But we should keep the want list short, simple and necessary.

In 1991, I needed desperately to move closer to my work. I knew I could make that happen myself, yet I wanted it to happen Christ's way. I had asked, begged, and finally been blocked on this issue. My peace was dissolving; my ability to help someone else through his or her stress was at an all-time low. God's timing was different than my time. So I waited. Even with my strained patience, I still knew God knew what was best for me—which He knew better than I. In January of 1993, we relocated to Aiken under God's perfect plan. He met my need. He settled my family there in keeping with the convenience I had begged for. He cleared me to be ready again to meet the needs of others.

We must have our own mental health to be useful to Christ. He desires all of us to live a no-hassle or low-hassle life. Why? Because He needs us to be emotionally free so we can focus on what Christ needs from us rather than what we need from Him.

[God] needs us to be emotionally free so we can focus on what He needs from us rather than what we need from Him.

Working in Harmony with Christ

As our faith grows, so does our ability to manage stress. Working in harmony with Christ lightens our load. We often think of our childhood as a carefree time, with a lack of responsibility and worry. That was a time when we relied on our parents. As adults, let us rely on our Heavenly Father. The power of positive thinking came out in the 1980s as the means to manage conflict and achieve success. However, the power of the Holy Spirit to manage conflict and success supersedes the power of our own thinking. This is more than an attitude; it is a supernatural process. We access powers we cannot see or understand through our simple faith in Christ.

Anna was a friend of mine, and I had desired, for years, for her to have the kind of peace that I knew. One day she relayed to me a most beautiful dream she had, which so clearly illustrates the necessity for the Holy Spirit in obtaining peace. In the morning, she awoke to remember the details of a dream where she saw an oil lamp with its light glowing brightly. The glass globe of the lamp was a colorful mosaic, but there was one mosaic piece missing. When she awoke and studied the dream, she came to realize that the lamp represented her inner peace, which had just one piece missing. She believed she would eventually know what it was that was holding her back from the complete peace and inner glow.

As she told me of this dream, I felt she was just steps away from the inner peace we had always talked about. Then, as she continued to share with me, she came to the complete understanding of the symbolism of this message. It was the personal acceptance of the Holy Spirit, and she was now ready to move forward toward that end, knowing that perfect peace would follow.

The symbolism of this dream so well represents the supernatural nature of the Holy Spirit's peace. No matter how hard we work to resolve all the different stresses in our lives, without the Holy Spirit, we are unable to achieve the peace that surpasses all understanding.

The more we trust Him, the more our faith grows in His ability to handle all things for us. Children seldom worry about food and clothes. Christ calls us to a childlike faith in His ability to handle our needs. In the book, *Timeless Wisdom* Mother Teresa once said, "Until you have nothing, you cannot believe you need nothing to live." In Mark 10:21 Christ said, "Take up your cross and follow me." He implied that we should leave all material things behind. Most of our "needs" are wants. With this bare-essential existence, we have fewer things to hassle our time, energy, and money. Clearly, though, in today's society, we have all gone in the opposite direction of the simplicity Christ recommended.

Truly, we have often been the beneficiary of great gifts—money, careers, nice homes, cars, and boats. Looking at the admirable life of Billy Graham, he has clearly tried to keep a multi-million-dollar ministry simple by accepting a normal salary, while living without extravagances. God has blessed his ministry. God does bless us, but the focus of our relationship needs to be what Christ wants from us, not what we want from Him. Want less … serve more. The Holy Spirit is free to direct our thoughts and situations in the right direction. Good decisions and wisdom lead to peace in the challenging events of life.

Over time, the confidence to trust Christ grows. You become a follower of Christ and a leader of men who can trust, delegate, and appreciate others for handling their jobs. Risk-taking seems easier when you have Christ on your side. When the Holy Spirit assures me, I take the risk, reach out, and listen for God's direction with a heightened awareness.

When God is quiet, I am still. Spiritual feelings guide us in proper decisions and directions. Some might say they work on a "hunch." That is what it feels like, yet the more you advance in hearing God's voice, the clearer your conscience reads the proper directions, and your emotions reflect that.

David said in Psalm 35:22, "Keep not silent; be not far from me." If this worked then, shouldn't we have gained a greater insight based on today's sophisticated world concerning how to think, seek, and work with the Holy Spirit? Be aware of your sixth sense. Use the Holy Spirit for guidance in decision-making, and use this ultimate sense of peace in fulfilling your missions on earth.

No matter how hard we work to resolve all the different areas of our life's stresses, without the Holy Spirit, we are unable to achieve the peace that surpasses all understanding.

… the focus of our relationship needs to be what Christ wants from us, not what we want from Him. Want less … serve more.

REVIEW & INTROSPECTION

CHAPTER 5: OBTAINING PEACE

WEEK 5

1. Rewrite the descriptions of peace cited within this chapter and then write your own description below them.

   _____

   _____

2. Why did God give us the Ten Commandments? If we lived by them, would they create more peace? Explain.

   _____

   _____

3. How can we deal with unforgiveness in our lives?

   _____

   _____

   *In the margin, list the names of family members and friends who have in some way wronged you. Pray over the list and ask God to help you to make the decision to forgive them today.

4. Why, in your opinion, does God say it would be harder for a rich man to enter the gates of heaven than for a camel to pass through the eye of a needle?

   _____

   _____

5. There were so many instances of peace described in this chapter! Why does God want *you* to live a peaceful life—like Colleen, my friend Caron, the prisoner of war?

   _____

   _____

6. What is the necessary "piece of the puzzle" to obtaining a peace that surpasses all understanding?

   _____

   _____

7. What is the significance of "want less … serve more"?

   _____

   _____

Scripture References: *What do these Scriptures mean to you personally?*
Philippians 4:7, 11

_____

Psalm 51:10

_____

Luke 12:31

_____

John 14:27

_____

BUILDING INTEGRITY

Integrity Fosters Belief

Integrity is a word that is significantly under-emphasized in sharing the good news of Jesus Christ as Savior. Without our integrity, nonbelievers will not believe what they are told. God calls us to live a life of high standards, strong morals, and again, integrity. He does this for two very essential reasons: to allow us to be believed by nonbelievers and to give to us the stress-free life so often described in the Bible.

For several years, I spent a great deal of time with my friend, Linda. We exercised, talked, laughed, and encouraged each other. For the first three years of our friendship, I had never shared Christ with her. Why? Because I was not led to do so.

One day, she opened the door for me to help her understand how to access Christ in her time of need. At that time, I shared with her my belief that all of us could hear God's voice, once we understood the concept. She was amazed. She said that no one else had been able to relay this information to her in such a way that she could accept it. She then proceeded to help me do something no one else had done for me—understand the value of integrity. Her basis for accepting this information from me was the relationship developed over our three years spent together. She had confirmed that I was a person of integrity. I could be trusted. I had never lied or misled her before, so there must be something to "this religion concept."

Wow! How had I lived thirty-six years and never understood that without integrity Christ cannot count on us to convince others that salvation through Him is the way to heaven?

Integrity Is Required if You Are to Be a Spokesperson

We have clearly seen the value of integrity through the fall of televangelists in the late 1980s. Men who had reached thousands of people, could no longer carry the message because they had lost their credibility. The standards God set are high. We are not perfect and cannot be perfect, but God returns more blessings than we can receive when we honor those standards in our lives.

Christ is more forgiving than man because He knows our hearts. He knows when we have sincerely repented by committing to improve our ways. He accepts our confessions and heightens our desires to do better next time. Man is less forgiving. Because man cannot see within another person's heart to know that the desire to change and improve is real, he has trouble overcoming doubts after trust has been crushed.

Prisoners who find Jesus are readily marked as fake. People who attempt to help others but carry addictions to drugs, sex, or gambling are discounted in their intentions to do good. A recovered child abuser's interest in helping other abusers stop their abuse is not likely to get that support because of his or her past failure. Integrity is required if you are to be a spokesperson.

The church is an easy target for claims of hypocrisy. Romans 3:23 ESV says, "All have fallen short of the glory of God." The truth is that every man is a hypocrite

Thought of the Week:
Christians have an obligation to demonstrate good judgment in what they say and do. Our integrity is viewed as the single most important means to determine if we are credible.

in the most literal sense. Jesus was the only man to show perfection. So what is the difference between a hypocrite and a Christian? The Christian admits his or her lack of perfection and strives to improve with the help of the Holy Spirit. Though only Christ knows our heart, with the help of the Holy Spirit, our friends can often see our attempts to do that which is right.

So what is the difference between a hypocrite and a Christian? The Christian admits his or her lack of perfection and strives to improve with the help of the Holy Spirit.

"Thou Shalt Not Judge Thine Clients"

As Christians, we seem to labor over the concept of judging. This was cleared up for me as a social worker in Social Work 101. Thou shalt not judge thine clients. Isn't it funny that nonreligious training taught me this concept so clearly? Jesus' examples not to judge are also very clear. He accepted a ruthless tax collector as a disciple. He welcomed everyone to His sermons, with no restrictions on dress or status. He held a conversation with a prostitute. He reached out to the disabled. He valued the penny of a poor widow. Then, He hung to die between two criminals, with whom He shared the plan of salvation.

So, why do we have such a hard time with judging? Because over the years we have set some standards that were designed to show respect for the Lord. In our good intentions, we have forgotten that the main purpose of our work is to bring all people to the Lord. I believe the Lord says, "I'll take you wherever you are," yet the church doesn't always do this.

Recently, a well-meaning Christian woman told me that she could not accept the casual wear allowed in many contemporary churches. She felt it was disrespectful. I found myself pondering what Jesus would think about this. It seems to me that whether people come in a mink coat and gold necklace or cut-off blue jeans, the Lord only cares about the condition of their heart, not what they wear on the outside. If He doesn't care, then why should we? A pastor called his newly formed church, "The church for the imperfect." That is really how it is meant to be.

... whether people come in a mink coat and gold necklace or cut-off blue jeans, the Lord only cares about the condition of their heart ...

I really do believe the Catholics have it right in the act of confession. They cannot come before the Lord without first facing their own transgressions.

Many believe that in heaven we will not stand to be judged by God but rather watch our life go before us like a home movie to account for one's good and bad actions. Christ's role there will be to comfort us in our pain as we see the pain we brought others or to praise us in watching our acts of service.

We should spend our time judging others, only ourselves. In Luke 6:37, we are told, "Judge not, and ye shall not be judged."

When Someone We Love Goes Astray

Throughout the Old and New Testament, we are told many times not to judge. So what do we do if we see someone we love go astray? In Galatians 6:1 NLT, we are told, "Dear Brothers, if a Christian is overcome by some sin, you who are godly should gently and humbly help him back onto the right path, remembering that next time it might be one of you who is in the wrong."

We seem to forget that it is with love that we bring people in. Several years ago, I overheard an employee, Teresa, telling another employee, "Your Jehovah Witness faith is nothing but a cult." As I watched his face, it was clear she had hurt him by what she had said. He turned and left. I said to Teresa, "Well, that should convert him to Christianity." In researching the Bible for Scriptures relating to judging, I found numerous references that simply state that we are "not to judge."

What responsibility do we have to bring out the sin of those in the church? In 1 Corinthians 5:12, Paul tells us to throw these men out. How could he say that? The most important part of that chapter is 1 Corinthians 5:3–5 where he tells us that the church should call a meeting and pray for God's will for these people, with the power of the Holy Spirit working in and through the body of Christ.

In my work throughout the years, there have been times when someone must be asked to leave for one reason or another. I have learned to make this the last resort. I pray God's will for the person, just as I pray for guidance in searching for new employees. I believe our only responsibility is to pray about these matters and let God do what He will. Only on the occasions where you feel the burden and direction to act should you directly approach the matter. In the workplace, just like in the church, there is a job of seeing that people do the jobs assigned to them and get the proper instructions. I have been amazed at how people can usually come to the proper conclusion on their own if counseled with kindness rather than a judgmental attitude. Only certain people have this gift of inspired communication. Unless after much prayer you feel you should act, then remain still and see His works being performed. We are all guilty of taking matters out of God's hands and into our own.

Realizing Paul wrote the Corinthian chapter on love, I don't believe he would ever have advocated judgmental, emotional attacks on another person. Someone once said, "A great manager is someone that can step on your toes and still leave your shoes shining." This requires a prepared and sensitive approach. Intercession and prayer are the keys to keeping good churches clean and the body of believers sensitive to God's direction. How have we become so prone to bringing the flaws of others to their attention? It is important to know and follow our own God-directed values so that we do not encourage others to stumble.

When others ask our advice or seek our counsel, we may give God's word without issue, but we must not spend our time judging others. We should continue to love them and use our greatest power—that of the Holy Spirit within us—and ask the Holy Spirit to convict them. Thus, our relationship with them can be preserved to help and not to hurt them. After all, most of us have to learn the hard lessons of life by experiencing them.

I strongly believe people are most easily led to believe in Christ through relationships with people that love them. Mothers, spouses, and close friends, are the greatest sources for sharing the pathway to heaven. We listen to people we trust and we trust that people we know would not lead us astray.

The Holy Spirit Gives Us An Edge

Everyone wonders at some point on the journey to acceptance of Christianity just how we can be so sure we are right. How do we know those of others faiths, such as Judaism, Buddhism, Islam, and New Age beliefs, are wrong? The difference comes with our ability to know Jesus personally—to hear His voice. When that level of faith is achieved, there is no longer room for doubt in our choice.

Religions that are faddish or cultish usually can be pinpointed by a common thread; they deviate from the standards, values, and principles in the Bible. Communal living that condones incest, polygamy, physical abuse, and substance abuse is clearly not operating within the principles that are consistent with salvation.

The difference comes with our ability to know Jesus personally–to hear His voice. When that level of faith is achieved, there is no longer room for doubt in our choice.

Yet many have fallen prey to these religious options because they allow and accept the pleasures of the earth in the name of their religion.

Integrity of the leadership is clearly questionable as they use power to rule and control rather than peace, love, and kindness.

In the Old-Testament days, the Ten Commandments set forth the standards. Before the Ten Commandments were given, the world strayed so far from integrity that God destroyed the world with a flood and found only Noah and his family to be worthy of preserving. Corruption had covered the world. God had lost His patience for people who promised to do better and yet never lived up to their word. The flood cleared the earth, and from Noah, a new generation began.

Later, Moses would receive the Ten Commandments to set forth the standards God expects those who love Him to follow. How much clearer could God have made it? The sins of those days are still rampant today. The earth has not been a perfect place. That privilege of knowing the perfect paradise is reserved for those "who will hear His voice and turn from their wicked ways," as stated in Isaiah 55:7 TLB. But turning from sin is still not an easy thing to do.

Today, however, while the Ten Commandments are a great guide, it was Jesus' entrance and exit of this world that changed the challenge. It is with the Holy Spirit that we have an edge. Jesus showed us how we could use the Holy Spirit to help overcome temptation.

First Corinthians 10:13 TLB states, "He will show you how to escape temptation's power so that you can bear up patiently against it." We can pray to Jesus, and He will close the door to temptation. Jesus was tempted for forty days in the desert and overcame it because of his ability to use the Holy Spirit and rely on the promises of God to stymie Satan's efforts. It sounds so easy, yet without the art of hearing His voice, we have not fully developed the means to stave off temptations.

Obedience Yields a "Clean Feeling"

All of us can think of times when we failed the test but more enjoyably can remember the sense of pleasure that comes from passing the test—the pride and the clean feeling of obedience. The most important reward of all is the peace we maintain within ourselves as we walk away from problems instead of creating them.

The most important reward of all is the peace we maintain within ourselves, as we walk away from problems instead of creating them.

As a former social worker and an employer for the past fifteen years, I have witnessed so much self-inflicted pain that comes from the poor decisions people make. The majority of today's stress comes from our own wrong acts and choices. Many families are destroyed by sex sins. Our health fails as we abuse our bodies. High-speed car accidents kill loved ones. Lying at work about a cover-up causes one to lose a job. A family is broken with financial excesses. Drug abuse sends a teenager to prison. Criminal acts cause pain to oneself, as well as to families and friends. "Softer" sins can remove our peace as well. Friendship can be lost over a small lie. Harsh words can cause pain to our spouse. Money misspent on frivolous activities can leave the checkbook out of kilter. The list of daily acts that cause stress goes on and on.

It is His desire that we not create problems for two reasons—to live stress free and to clear out burdens so we can serve Him.

God called us to His higher standards because He loves us. He hurts when we hurt. He told us how to make it easier. It is His desire that we not create problems for those same two reasons—to live stress free and to clear out burdens so we can serve Him.

Having our own needs met is important because we cannot be free to help Him when we are sad, hungry, confused, or feeling unloved. But until we trust Him to carry our burdens for us, we are stymied by our unbelief.

The Bible is full of reminders to cast our cares upon Him. My favorite is, "But even the very hairs of your head are numbered. Fear not, therefore; ye are of more value than many sparrows" (Luke 12:7).

God's intelligence is so far beyond our ability to grasp or understand that we overlook how much He can and will do for us.

We Can Do All Things through Christ

With our integrity intact, He can give us the pleasure of helping to carry out His work. He calls us to these values for our benefit as well as His. I have often heard it said, "You can't outgive the Lord." If we live up to His standards, He gives us peace. We carry out His work; we receive the pleasure of helping others. This is a good deal, a fair trade. It sounds so easy, but the day-to-day trials seem overwhelming and we forget to look up and say, "Help!" That's all it takes. We must keep our integrity.

We live up to His standards, and He gives us peace.

With each test we pass, we are then stronger for the next encounter. We are more prepared to take on the pressure. Not all our pain is self-inflicted. Sometimes circumstances arise that have nothing to do with wrong judgments. A child is hit by a car. A house is lost to lightning. An illness intrudes on the family. A child is born with a birth defect. A young spouse dies, leaving an uncertain future for the remaining spouse, and in some cases, children. It is during these hardships that our chance to build integrity comes.

It is paramount to go forward in service despite hardships. Crisis situations can motivate our belief. These instances also elevate our character. We gain greater patience, stronger faith, stamina to recover, and a greater awareness of others' love for us. These trials, whether self-inflicted or by natural causes, prepare us to walk forward through the hardship with confidence in the ability to endure all things through Christ. Romans 5:3 TLB says, "We can rejoice too when we run into trials for we know that they are good for us—they help us learn to be patient. And patience develops strength of character in us and helps us trust God more each time we use it until our hope and faith are strong and steady."

Crisis situations can motivate our belief. These instances also elevate our character. We gain greater patience, stronger faith, stamina to recover, and a greater awareness of others' love of for us.

At the 1997 Academy Awards, Cuba Gooding Jr. was awarded an Oscar as Best Supporting Actor for his role in the movie *Jerry McGuire*. With great enthusiasm, he began to announce persons to whom he was grateful. As the music became louder in an attempt to end his thirty-second allotted time, he responded by becoming louder and louder. Over the music, with a tremendous smile, and all the life one could own, he said, "Thank you, Lord, for all you put me through." It was an Academy Award moment. While I have no idea what his personal trials might have been, his response mirrored that of a person who could appreciate growth through challenge.

The prolific apostle Paul told us to be thankful for the trials and the troubles we see, for they are used to build up our faith. Those persons who can handle challenges with integrity are admired on earth. Parents who allow their children to work through their own problems and suffer the consequences, know these tribulations build character. These challenges prepare us for the harder tests.

The prolific apostle Paul told us to be thankful for the trials and the troubles we see, for they are used to build up our faith.

Jesus showed us integrity under pressure. On the cross, He looked up in the sky and said, "Father, forgive them for they know not what they do" (Luke 23:34 ESV). He gave His enemies the benefit of the doubt. He owned no hate. He suffered physical pain, public ridicule, and the emotional loss of leaving. His mother and friends on earth showed us how it was done. His exit carried every possible grain of integrity, forgiveness, and love to everyone in that moment.

We lose our integrity when we can't forgive others. Again, though, it is harder for us because we do not know the hearts of other men. Can we trust this person again? Mostly, we base our opinions on watching other people's track record. Do they keep their promises? Do they admit their wrongs to us? When they don't, can we overlook it? Jesus showed us to turn the other cheek. Today the corporate world is full of "get-even" behavior. Integrity is built on forgiving and forgetting. In today's society, we forget to forgive.

Today the corporate world is full of "get-even" behavior. Integrity is built on forgiving and forgetting.

Integrity Is a Lifestyle

More than anything else, our integrity is based on our lifestyle. Christians have an obligation to demonstrate good judgment in what they say and do. Our representation is viewed as the single most important means to determine if we are credible.

Our actions, decisions, and attributes convey our moral code. This is where the Holy Spirit's role assists us. As the Spirit intensifies our conscience, our standards improve. As we grow in Christ, we are less tolerant of our faults and less compromising in our integrity. This behavior alone can be an indication of the growth of the Holy Spirit's presence in us.

As children, we told lies, took a playmate's toy, or ignored someone's needs. As adults, we learn to expect more of ourselves. The light that the Holy Spirit shines on us is used to show us our flaws and flows so clearly that we cannot ignore our own wrongs. The urge to rebuild hurt relationships or correct a wrong causes such a burden that we must handle to restore our peace.

"I don't care what people think," is not something we can say anymore if we really care about our integrity. We must care so that our image and reputation go untarnished. For the first time, I realized how priceless our reputation is and how quickly we can lose our integrity by association with those who don't carry our same values. Every effort must be made to rectify relationships, explain decisions, and clarify behaviors. Precautions must be taken to avoid wrong impressions. In other words, we are accountable to our fellow man if we want to remain unwavering in our integrity.

Some years ago my mother sent me a check for $100 with "good daughter payment" written on the memo. I sat down to write her a letter ...

> *Dear Mama,*
> *This year has been a real challenge to me, to my character, and to my faith.*
> *And the outcome has been two beautiful results. I have never felt the power*
> *of God stronger than in dealing with these matters. His words, His voice, and*
> *His peace have all strengthened me. And the other most important gain is the*
> *realization of how proud I am of whom I am, who I have become in Christ—a*
> *person with a clear mind for what's right and wrong. I realized I am the person*
> *I am because of you. Through years when I challenged your thinking, you stood*

strong in your beliefs. It's taken me thirty-three years to appreciate you as deeply as I do today. I know I have lived a life of good morals with nothing to be ashamed of. God has forgiven my mistakes, and my faith has kept me on a path that has brought me much happiness. The good daughter payment came when I needed to hear that. I have been unable to cash the check, since the words meant more than the money. Thank you for all the time you have taken with me to teach me right and wrong. I now know, through Scott, how much is required to ensure he is a good boy. I love you, Mom.

Love, Jane

Humility is a vital character-building trait required to carry out God's work. Being the "bigger man," in terms of personal pride and integrity, is a posture we must take even when we don't deserve to be the one to make the reconciliation. Humility means giving up our self-centered thinking so that we can humble ourselves before the Lord. In other words, we become servants in our minds. Why? Because it builds integrity, restores relationships, and maintains the peace.

The company we keep is quickly assessed as a reflection of ourselves. Jesus was nonjudgmental toward everyone and He was open to be a friend to all. Jesus could handle temptations and peer pressure. We are often not so strong, so in order to reduce temptation and decrease the risk of error, choosing good company makes building integrity easier. As we rise up in our ability to resist temptation, we are freer to reach out to those with lesser standards as a means to be helpful and useful to God's work.

Integrity Allows a Higher Level of Service

Jesus said it would not be easy as He prepared the disciples for their work. It is not any easier today. But the rewards of integrity carry their own earthly gain. Others can think well of us and we can enjoy the sense of obedience to God. Just as a child feels pleasure from pleasing his or her parent(s), so we, too, feel pleasure from pleasing the Father.

As we build integrity, we prepare ourselves to serve at higher levels. While the temptations do not end, Christ's messenger, the Holy Spirit, works to protect us from falling prey to the temptations. First Corinthians 10:13 TLB says:

For you can trust God to keep the temptations from becoming so strong that you can stand up against it, for He has promised this and will do what He says. He will show you how to escape temptation's power so that you can bear up patiently against it.

A Lack of Integrity Causes Separation

God calls us to build integrity and avoid sin for another critical reason: so we can hear His voice. An older Baptist minister said it best when he said, "When we be's bad, God, He be's real quiet." It is a Christian tenet that sin separates us from the Father. In Isaiah 59 (Living Bible Paraphrased) it says, "Listen now! The Lord isn't too weak to save you. And He isn't getting deaf! He can hear you when you call! But the trouble is that your sins have cut you off from God."

Also in Mark 11:25, we are told to forgive anyone against whom we are holding a grudge so our Father in heaven may forgive us. We are to do this before we pray

God calls us to build integrity and avoid sin for another critical reason: so we can hear His voice.

so our prayers will be answered. He cannot be a part of our wrong decisions. He leaves us in charge of ourselves, whether to look to Him or to look to the choices of the world. We can remove sin immediately by confession to God, who forgives and forgets. This is vital to keeping the two-way communication link open. He does not leave us. He simply waits with open arms for us to return to Him.

Many times, though, He will use opportunities on Earth to help us turn from our mistakes and sins. The Holy Spirit is a great help, as guilt is painful, stressful, and burdensome. Consequences from sin sometimes are enough to turn us back to Him. But nonetheless, He waits. He waits for you to come to Him. Just the thought of losing access to Christ has helped me pass over disastrous decisions and actions. That was what He had in mind.

He separates Himself as a deterrent so we will think our actions through more carefully. Once we have become so dependent on Him for decision-making, we don't want to lose the communication. He has given us another great promise in Hebrews 13:5 ESV when He said, *"I will never leave thee nor forsake thee."*

He will, however, wait quietly on us to call out to Him. As He said to me in my need for action to start my relocation to Aiken, "I'm as close as I have ever been." It was not God who moved; it was me who had moved away from Him. The pain He feels when we separate from Him is like the loss of a close friend; and so He waits. When we return to Him, He takes us back time and time again. The beloved song "The Savior Is Waiting" by Ralph Carmichael reminds me of that.

> *Time after time He has waited before, And now He is waiting again,*
> *To see if we're willing to open the door. Oh, won't you let Him come in?*
> *Receive Him and all of His sorrow will end. Within our heart He'll abide.*

Only Jesus could take our rejection, yet stand there ready for us to return. He cares about our peace and our ability to serve Him. Our level of integrity parallels our ability to fulfill our assignments on Earth. Prayer, the tool to communicate with Christ, must be well-developed so we can engage in two-way communication. Prayer is simply talking with God. "With" is the key word here. Knowing how to efficiently and effectively talk with God helps us to accomplish the work He has given to us.

The pain He feels when we separate from Him is like the loss of a close friend; and so He waits. When we return to Him, He takes us back time and time again.

REVIEW & INTROSPECTION

CHAPTER 6: BUILDING INTEGRITY

WEEK
6

1. As Christians, it is important that we live lives that are pleasing to God. What are the two reasons God calls us to a life of integrity?

2. List below some of Jesus' examples of my lessons in Social Work 101, "Thou shalt not judge thine clients"

3. Instead of judging others, according to Galatians 6:1, what should we do if we see someone we love go astray?

4. It is with love, not judgment, that we can convert people to Christianity. Have you ever loved anyone into the faith? Or is there anyone you can show love to in order to help him or her find Christ?

5. *Crisis situations can motivate our belief.* What situation in your life, although difficult, elevated your character?

6. How can associating with those who don't carry your same values affect you negatively?

7. Re-read the words to "The Savior Is Waiting." How do they make you feel?

8. Define "prayer."

Take a moment to pray right now before you move on to chapter 7.

Scripture References: *What do these Scriptures mean to you personally?*

Romans 3:23

___

Luke 6:37

___

First Corinthians 10:13

___

III. LEARNING TO LISTEN

Week 7   Believing Him for Direction 51

Week 8   Recognizing His Voice 61

Week 9   Growing in Clarity 75

BELIEVING HIM FOR DIRECTION

Christ's Prayers Were Answered

Jesus scored 100 percent when it came to having His prayers answered. How did He do this? He knew how to hear the voice of God. The idea behind Christian growth is to model Jesus' life. He was sent to save us and to show us that man could, while walking on earth, overcome temptation, care for others , and mentally connect with the Father God. He prayed for things consistent with the will of God because He knew the Father's thoughts through His own mind and spirit. All His needs were met, yet He owned nothing material when His earthly existence came to an end on the cross.

The Bible is complete, with texts that confirm it was God's design for us to work in conjunction with Christ in order to pray His will into happening. In 1 Corinthians 2, Paul explained this clearly, much more clearly than I have ever found it expressed elsewhere. The last line—a rhetorical question in nature—makes the point when it states, "Who would ever believe we have with (us) the very thoughts and mind of Christ, and have with us the power to move the hands of God by prayer." That thought has captivated my imagination, motivated my desire to increase my understanding, and thus, heightened my own spiritual power.

Access to the Power of God

As a child, I suffered during my elementary school years with great shyness, so it was often difficult to make friends and share my opinions. My family was actually surprised by my public shyness, because at home I was bold, opinionated, determined, and mature for my age. Yet, it was this shyness that allowed me to spend time alone pondering what other people's comments really meant. I was always fascinated with what others thought and why. In spiritual matters, I was constantly searching for deeper meanings and clearer understanding. *Why would the Bible tell us the message in James 1:5–6 TLB?*

> If you want to know what God wants you to do, ask Him and He will gladly tell you, for He is always ready to give a bountiful supply of wisdom to all who ask Him. If you don't ask with faith, don't expect the Lord to give you any solid answer.

Why would Paul, in 1 Corinthians 12:10, discuss the gifts, which included prophecy, to know the future? Why would God make a plan to know us and love us, yet not talk to us?

My search went on from early elementary school until the birth of my son—a crisis period that changed my spiritual life. God displayed Himself to me in a stronger two-way communication method than I had ever experienced. This life-changing experience left me appreciative and motivated me to grow in my abilities to access the power of God for others, others who I believed would need me in the future. But more than anything else, the spared life of my son left me forever

Thought of the Week:
In other words, if you do not believe you can hear from God, then you will not. The turning point is when you open yourself to the possibility that He can and will share with you.

Why would Paul in 1 Corinthians 12:10 discuss the gifts, which included prophecy, to know the future? Why would God make a plan to know us and love us, yet not talk to us?

indebted on earth to express to others that God's voice is real and can be accessed by all those with the faith and desire to hear. Faith is well defined in Hebrews 11:1.

But what is faith? It is the confident assurance that something we want is going to happen. It is the feeling of certainty that what we hope for is waiting for us, even though we cannot see it ahead.

Jesus was able to heal a blind man. How could this happen? Jesus said, "Because of your faith, it will happen" (Matt. 9:29 NLT) To hear God's voice, we must have a confidence that will happen for us (Heb. 11:1). Our thoughts are limited because we have not yet heard it, but we have not heard His voice because we did not believe. In other words, if you do not believe you can hear from God, then you will not. The turning point is when you open yourself to the possibility that He can and will share with you.

Hearing God's Voice

It is acceptable to talk of His answered prayers in soft terminology. *"He touched me"* is often used to express the feeling of the Holy Spirit upon us. *"I was led to believe"* is used to share confessions of thoughts that were divine. *"He answered my prayer"* is used to share beliefs that an act or a coincidence carried out by man was motivated by Christ through prayer. Within the informed, experienced, and mature Christian, these indirect references carry the same meaning as, *"I heard God's voice."*

This concept of God's plan to answer prayer is the toughest part of religion to explain. In 1 Corinthian 2:13 TLB, Paul states support of how hard a concept this is to convey, as he credits the Holy Spirit for giving him the words when he writes:

> In telling you about these gifts we have even used the very words given to us by the Holy Spirit, not words that we as men might choose. So we use the Holy Spirit's words to explain the Holy Spirit's facts.

Hearing the voice of God is an abstract, personally unique process that grows only with desire. It is lived out by practice and the faith to believe God can and will talk to us.

As executive director of a large, nonprofit health care and rehabilitation facility for fourteen years, I had seen it grow from twelve employees to almost 250 people. One of the enjoyable tasks of my job is to take abstract work, such as "how to start a hospice program," and break down the effort into a clear understanding of how to accomplish the task. This often includes summarizing a huge amount of information, clarifying steps, and training people in the process. I love to take an abstract matter and make it clear.

It is the ultimate challenge to take the art of hearing God's voice, which may seem like an abstract concept, and make it clear and applicable to readers. Only through the guidance of the Holy Spirit could this work be completed. Fear of public ridicule and lack of clear teaching are hindrances to this process. Yet without the desire to grow and the faith to believe, God's voice will not be heard.

Some years ago, my cousin Jeana, age twenty-two, suffered a head injury after being thrown from a three-wheel vehicle. The back of her head hit a telephone pole. My Aunt Mary and I visited her after Christmas at a rehabilitation center in North Carolina. Even though she could not verbally respond, I realized within minutes of being with her that she could hear and understand the communication around her. Nurses came in and talked about her in a friendly manner. Visitors came in and asked each other how she was doing. With my background in rehabilitation, I felt she could communicate with us if we helped her. She could definitely respond to yes or no questions accurately. I found if I thought hard enough, I could word most anything to get her response. I set up a number system for her so she could communicate with us. For example, I told her to raise three fingers for a tissue; I played tic-tac-toe with her by yes or no responses, and I asked her how she felt by offering word options to her.

She was clearly frustrated that she could not communicate with us verbally. She wanted to convey many things to us, and it was hard to watch her suffering in her frustration. For the hour we visited, I talked with her directly, and we accomplished two-way communication. I left feeling she would continue to improve.

Days later while I was driving in my car, I had this clear understanding; we treat the Lord like He is in a coma. We believe He can hear us and that He understands what we are saying, yet we do not believe He can communicate back to us in any way. In thinking of this and remembering my cousin's frustration, I thought of Christ. He has so much that He desires to tell us. He knows how to direct our success, our happiness, and our decisions. He desires to use us to bring joy to others and thus, receive it in return. Yet, we leave Him helpless to connect. We talk at Him and about Him, not believing He can talk back.

He knows how to direct our success, our happiness, and our decisions. He desires to use us to bring joy to others and thus receive it in return. Yet, we leave Him helpless to connect.

The Holy Spirit Motivates Desire

In watching my cousin's frustrations and magnifying that millions of times to represent the believers who treat Him like He is in a coma, I felt great sadness. On the other hand, when Christ finds Christians who desire to develop the art of two-way communication, then the excitement begins. He desires that all Christians will grow and develop so that He may provide for their every need. Many Christians are content to accept Jesus as Savior and live morally "acceptable" lives. According to most Protestant Christian denominations, belief in Jesus as Savior will reserve your seat in heaven. When a person limits his or her desire to this level of service, then at that it will rest. Desire is the key word here.

The Holy Spirit motivates desire, and if we continue to seek Him out, the desire will grow. So, for most Christians, it is a journey, growing as we walk in service. Some travel the journey quickly, others more slowly.

A curiosity to understand spiritual matters is a part of our human nature. The unknown intrigues us, and we have a void until we begin to find the answers in our naturally inquiring minds. Since many believers accepted Jesus Christ as Savior at a young age, often the knowledge quest grows as one matures. Many Christian faiths believe the Holy Spirit enters us at the time of acceptance of Jesus Christ as the incarnate Son of God. Jesus' life exemplifies this idea with the baptism conducted by John the Baptist. In Mark 1:10 (TLB), at the Baptism of Jesus by John the Baptist, it was recorded, "And straightway coming up out of the water, he saw the heavens opened, and the Spirit like a dove descending upon Him."

While we are beginners in our understanding of the faith, the Holy Spirit motivates us softly to desire to know the Lord. He serves as our conscience, helping us do good deeds and God's work. He intensifies our consciousness. The Holy Spirit works by sparking our emotions. Then our brain translates this feeling into intelligent thoughts to share with others. Our body uses our mouth to translate it

The Holy Spirit works by sparking our emotions. Then our brain translates this feeling into intelligent thoughts to share with others. Our body uses our mouth to translate it into audible words.

into audible words. Study that sentence carefully. It is the clearest description I have for explaining the two-way communication process. Within us are components of emotion (spirit), mentality (mind), and the physical (body). The emotional component is where the Holy Spirit first responds to us, as it is the easiest component with which to connect. Later come mental and physical means as we grow.

The emotional component is the beginning basis for the work of the Holy Spirit. He can connect with us in this realm even without the understanding of the two-way communications. In church, after a good sermon, we leave "inspired." Often we feel "touched" or our spirits are "lifted." In another direction, we leave church, or prayer time, and our feeling of conviction is intensified and our pain heightened.

"Upon Us" versus "In Us"

There are efforts the Holy Spirit can perform without our knowledge. Before we accept the Holy Spirit, He is considered "upon" us, gently nudging us to allow Him inside us for the gain of our full salvation. Once we have accepted Jesus, the Holy Spirit is then "in" us and available to enable us to grow and serve at the level at which we so desire.

For years, people have written poems, created other great works of art, arrived at remarkable philosophical thoughts, discovered enlightening natural truths, and considered themselves "inspired" at the time. Even without acknowledgment, the Holy Spirit can heighten our emotions and create wonderful works through us. But it is amazing what can be accomplished when we acknowledge Him. This inspiration is spoken of by Paul in Ephesians 3:20 TLB:

> Now glory be to God who by His mighty power at work within us is able to do far more than we would ever dare to ask or even dream of infinitely beyond our highest prayers, desires, thoughts, or hopes.

Initiative to grow in this understanding of Christ is motivated by the Holy Spirit. Some individuals feel this more clearly than others, just as some persons are very sensitive to the feelings of others and some are not. The growth process takes time—time spent in studying God's Word, time spent among other believers who can explain and reinforce the thinking, and most importantly, time spent in prayer seeking the Father.

The growth process takes time—time spent in studying God's Word, time spent among other believers who can explain and reinforce the thinking, and most importantly, time spent in prayer seeking the Father.

To Know and Love God

The feeling of love for the Father has to be intensely personal. I can say I love my earthly father, but until you know Him, you cannot make the same claim. It is a relationship. Here we go again into the abstract.

How can you love someone you have never talked to? My husband loved his great-grandmother very much. Over the years, he has talked of her so many times, shared stories of her unselfishness, talked of her values and humor. I feel as though I know and loved her through him.

The Bible was designed to assist us in knowing God, Jesus, and the Holy Spirit through its accounts and writings. Since Jesus was the only one of these three—the Trinity—who walked on earth as a man, it is easier for us to relate to Him. The Bible shares so many historical accounts of His kindness, cleverness, and compassion for others. Just listening to what the disciples said makes us admire Jesus greatly.

Jesus no longer walks the earth as a man. In perfect planning for His absence, God prepared for the Holy Spirit to come and give us the same access to His thoughts and mind that the disciples had. Unlike the disciples, we cannot touch Jesus, hug Him, or witness Him physically performing miracles. He knew this. He knew it would be harder to know Him. He admitted it when He said in John 20:29, "Thomas because thou hast seen me, thou has believed; blessed are they that have not seen and yet have believed."

The Holy Spirit works through our emotions, giving us a greater sense of love for others and for Christ. When we commit the time and energy to grow, the Holy Spirit will help us get to know the Father. Understanding and accepting the Holy Spirit helps us gain mental abilities.

Again, this may happen without one's knowledge or acceptance of the acts of the Holy Spirit—those inspired thoughts, dreams, or coincidences. However, the real results in understanding the power of prayer begin when we truly believe these are motivated by Christ in us, not by ourselves.

Why does Christ want credit? Mostly because He is the source for nonbelievers to believe. The miracles performed by Jesus during His stay on Earth were blatant demonstrations of His power. News carried quickly in a time of history when there were no telephones, televisions, or newspapers.

Again, Christ knew it would be hard to believe in Him when He was gone, according to John 20:29. He is dependent upon us to share His good news. The emotional, mental, and physical means are all accessible by one-way communication. It's when we desire to take these inquiring minds of ours to new heights that we enter the two-way communication realm.

He can talk to us. He is as real as you desire Him to be. Yet, we treat Him like He is in that coma. The power to see other people's problems solved and a life of peace for us rests in our ability to know Him.

It's when we desire to take these inquiring minds of ours to new heights that we enter the two-way communication realm.

He's as Real as You Want Him to Be

Christ can be more intensely real to us during a crisis than at any other time. Think of examples in our own life—through the death of a loved one, family conflict, health concerns, unemployment, infertility, addictions, and life's failures. It is most often through these experiences that God's help is needed.

During this time of peak desire, He makes Himself real to us, as never before. We then realize a greater level of faith, as a result of our dependence on Him. In more exact terms, at the news of an illness, our faith can be measured by prayer requests. If one asks for a good night's rest to strengthen one for recovery versus an outright request for healing, this can be an indication of the level of faith involved. The weaker the faith, the weaker the request. In other words, people pray for what they *think* God can do for them. As we grow in our understanding, our initiatives to pray for our wishes to come to pass are replaced by prayers more in harmony with God's will. Nonetheless, the crisis can motivate the desire. Christ will seize every opportunity to make Himself real to you. But you must be the initiator. He is ready when you call. He cannot come to you without your permission, acceptance, and desire.

Christ will seize every opportunity to make Himself real to you. But you must be the initiator ... He cannot come to you without your permission, acceptance and desire.

Over the years, I can honestly say the Lord has taken my shyness away so that I can speak boldly for Him. My experiences and challenges have developed my ability to hear God's voice. While I am still a calm person, the adventures surrounding me are exciting as I strive to submit to Christ for my direction—from whom to marry, to simple tasks like grocery shopping, to how to negotiate large contracts for my company.

I am thankful for the people who have crossed my path and shared their knowledge with me. Mostly I am thankful for understanding the Holy Spirit as a resource made available to all followers of Christ to be able to communicate with the Master.

Why is it when we talk to God it is okay, but when He talks to us we're nuts? ... However, in the Bible it is clearly recorded that God spoke.

Why is it when we talk to God it is okay, but when He talks to us, we're nuts? On the CBS network show, *Touched by an Angel*, the story plots revolved around this basic reaction. This is because basically we have silenced the public acceptance of hearing God's voice. However, in the Bible, it is clearly recorded that God spoke.

And "God Said!"

Well, what did He say? Many things, as the phrase "God said" is stated 558 times from Genesis to Revelations and in seventeen of the sixty-six books within the Bible. Was it difficult in biblical times to believe that these persons had actually heard from God? Probably so, but their track records proved them right. They were men and women of integrity and wisdom and were greatly respected by their people. Much of what God said in the Old Testament served as a reminders of the commandments, warnings of punishments, and encouragements to His chosen people. God's voice in those times—just as today—took different forms.

People of the Old and New Testament did not have the written Word of the Bible that we have today. Fortunately for us, the Bible is one way God speaks directly to us. Prior to the written word, God spoke to His people through supernatural encounters. David said in Psalm 119:105, "Thy word is a lamp unto my feet and a light unto my path." He must have been speaking of an encounter with the Lord.

Adam experienced an appearance of God in the Garden of Eden that startled him. Sin was the subject of the encounter in Genesis 3:9–10. Later, Moses was in God's presence, with the burning bush, for God to tell him of His plan to deliver His people to the Promised Land. Just like people today, Moses' worst fear was that the people of Israel would not believe he had heard God's actual voice. A rod was provided to Moses to demonstrate the miracle of the rod changing into a snake, and then back again, so people would accept Moses' power to hear God's voice. In the next account, God spoke to the people of Israel as a reminder of the Ten Commandments. This time, as they heard the Lord's voice themselves, they believed it was God, and it was reported in Deuteronomy 5:24, "We have seen this day that God doth talk with man and He liveth."

We have seen this day that God doth talk with man and He liveth.
—*Deuteronomy 5:24*

God called Samuel's name in his sleep, and it was so real Samuel ran to Eli, his priest. After three times, Eli advised Samuel this was God calling. Samuel was told in a vision he would become a prophet (see 1 Sam. 3:1–14).

Elijah heard God's voice after being awakened by an angel. God shared with him that he would be a prophet (see 1 Kings 19:16).

Isaiah and Ahaz were both able to hear God's voice. Ahaz received the prophecy of the coming of the birth of Jesus through a vision (see Isa. 7:12–17).

Ezekiel had visions and heard God's voice regarding the sins of the people (see Ezek. 2:2).

The New Testament accounts revolve around Jesus' ability to hear God's voice, as in Mark 1:11:

> And there came a voice from Heaven saying "Thou art my beloved son in whom I am well pleased."

In Matthew 17, we are told that while at the top of a mountain, where Jesus had taken Peter, James, and John, Moses and Elijah appeared with Jesus after He was transfigured before their eyes. God's voice was heard reaffirming that Jesus was His beloved son.

> Saul, who persecuted the followers of Jesus, was on his way to Damascus for the purpose of persecuting more Christians when he was stopped on the road with a light from Heaven so strong that it blinded his vision for three days. In this light was Jesus and He spoke to Saul, "Saul, Saul, why do you persecute me?" Saul asked "Who are you?" Jesus replied "I am Jesus whom you are persecuting. Now get up and go into the city and you will be told what you must do." The transformation of Saul into the apostle Paul was the outcome of this encounter (Acts 9:3-7 ESV).

Joseph received a message from God, through an angel in a dream, to flee Egypt to spare Jesus from Herod's massacre of young boys (see Matt. 2:13).

Mary received reassurance of the virgin birth, through the appearance of an angel delivering God's voice (see Luke 1:28–38). In addition, Joseph was reassured of the virgin birth by an angel through a dream (see Matt. 1:20–21).

These are just some of the accounts of direct communication in the Old and New Testament. Hebrews tells us of the new system that would come after Jesus' death. Hebrews 4:7 ESV says, "Today if you will hear his voice, harden not your hearts."

God spoke very specifically to Noah about His expectations. Few people today have been called to demonstrate the Noah level of faith in hearing God's voice. We are told through biblical interpretation that people doubted Noah's efforts, but he was confident in his understanding of God's instructions.

In all these accounts, it is evident that a system to communicate with God has been vital to the Lord for carrying out His plans on Earth. In order to do His work, we must be able to share thoughts. No good system of communication is one way.

David said in the Psalms, "Oh that you would hear Him calling you today and come to Him" (Ps. 95:7 ESV). Doesn't it seem just as necessary to hear from God today as it was in biblical times?

In all these accounts, it is evident that a system to communicate with God has been vital to the Lord for carrying out His plans on Earth.

What could be more important than communication when we are trying to get to know God?

REVIEW & INTROSPECTION

CHAPTER 7: BELIEVING HIM FOR DIRECTION

WEEK

7

1. What, according to the text, is the definition of "faith"?

    _____

    _____

2. Which of the following attributes are required to hear God's voice?

    Faith   Salvation   Baptism   Fellowship

    Forgiveness   Works   Spiritual Gifts   Desire

3. In your own words, explain the two-way communication process between Christians and the Holy Spirit.

    _____

    _____

4. What three activities should a beginner Christian desiring to grow in the understanding of Christ spend time doing?

    _____

    _____

5. Recall a time in your personal life when Christ was undeniably real to you—as real as He was to Adam in the garden, Moses at the burning bush, or Saul on the road to Damascus. Explain.

    _____

    _____

6. Would you consider your level of clarity in communication with Christ to be beginner, intermediate, or advanced? Explain.

    _____

    _____

7. How did God communicate with the following? Review their stories in the Bible to refresh your faith.

    Adam (Gen. 3:1–24) _____

    _____

    Moses (Ex. 3:1–6) _____

    _____

Samuel (1 Sam. 3:114) _____

_____

Ahaz & Isaiah (Isa. 7:12–17) _____

_____

Ezekiel (Ezek. 2:1–10) _____

_____

Saul (Acts 9:1–7) _____

_____

Joseph (Matt. 2:18–24) _____

_____

Mary (Luke 1:26–38) _____

_____

Thomas (John 20:24–29) _____

_____

The Disciples at the Mount of Transfiguration (Matt .17:1-13) _____

_____

RECOGNIZING HIS VOICE

God Answers Prayer

God desires to be heard today. The more I credit Him for His acts, the more He can do. It is a cycle that magnifies itself with each of my personal experiences. Someone recently asked me how I learned all of this. The answer is that the Holy Spirit told me. Left on my own for most of the journey, I learned to ask for explanations to this pondering.

The truth is that my IQ is average. Very few people wanted to tell me how to hear God's voice. My life's experiences have been mostly limited to two small towns in South Carolina, and my greatest attribute is an above-average dose of common sense. So, using my common sense and my naturally growing love of Christ, I set out to gain this power the Bible addresses over and over. If it said we could have all our prayers answered, I wanted to be able to help others when they needed me.

As a social worker, I spent the first three years of my career listening to people who hurt. I wanted to help them. Over time, I realized the answers were not within reach for many of these people because the real answers to our needs are through spiritual awakening. As I have grown in this understanding, the Holy Spirit heightens my desire to share with others the "how to" of this abstract process.

The accounts of this section represent how anyone could learn to recognize the voice of God. To each person, He will reveal Himself in different situations and through different acts. No two experiences ever seem the same, even for me. But the concept is steady. He uses people, both believers and nonbelievers to help get our attention, to tell us that He is available. He is waiting for your initiative to allow Him to show you what He can do.

How He Communicates

Physical, mental, and spiritual acts are the three means by which communication is received by our body, mind, and soul. Again, each experience involving God's voice usually displays a dominant means of communication, but all three parts are involved in order to understand God's intentions.

While each experience that a person defines as answered prayer can come in various means of communication, usually they all involve some element of the body, mind, and soul working together to understand how that prayer was answered. The level of faith from which we operate dictates the depth and clarity with which we can hear God's voice. The means by which Christ brings His message to us varies with each experience.

Physical communications are "acts." They are actual encounters by other persons through whom the spoken or written words of God's message are brought to us. Throughout our lives, we can often see God's work take place through acts involving coincidences that are all so perfectly timed it is impossible not to attribute them to some greater power. These can involve acts such as the words of other people, specific deeds, or even lyrics, poems, and Scriptures that carry a message resolving earthly entanglements. Often, God's voice is relayed through human voices. For

Thought of the Week:
The Holy Spirit will be your guide. All you must do is ask and believe and your daily communications will clarify themselves to a point of greater service.

The level of faith from which we operate dictates the depth and clarity with which we can hear God's voice.

many Christians, we pray and God answers. This means of communication is often recognized by our statements, such as, "God opened the door." An "opportunity" is made clear to us by an act. For example, a job is offered. A new friend is found to share our loneliness. An apartment is mysteriously vacant on the day we need a new residence. A rainy day cancels our trip, and only later do we find that our child needs us to help him or her with a personal crisis that very day.

These are the initiatives most often recognized by those whose communicational ability is one-way. All we have to do is pray for our need and the rest will be resolved. Indeed, this works, especially for those whose belief holds that Christ cannot talk to us; He simply paves the way. But we must watch and wait for the door to open, putting aside our own inclination to open doors ourselves.

Acts of others that involve words of comfort and direction at just the right time in God's perfect timing are another physical means of God's communication. In such cases, God answers through a person's voice. The message is obvious, and we are filled with amazement. God's voice is often relayed through the human voice, as it was through the wonderful, kind woman who comforted me after Scott's birth. The timing of her entrance into my life could not have been more perfect. Through acts like these, God's voice is confirmed to us. Many times a spouse unknowingly directs the destiny of the other as he or she offers just the right advice without knowing the issue. At breakfast, the husband tells the wife, "You will know what to do today with your boss. Someone will help you know the time to approach him about your concern." Then sure enough, a colleague comes to schedule such an event.

We can even amaze ourselves at our ability to know what to say to someone in pain. Without thinking, our words offer the exact solution. For example, a friend approaches a new businessman with an opportunity the same day the man had resolved to surrender his attempts at his new business to God. The act was the vote of confidence necessary to continue on the path God had chosen.

We find direction not only by opportunities and others' words but also though written words. God's intention becomes clear in poems and lyrics that minister to our needs in such a way that they are deemed more than sheer coincidence. A man who was struggling with the temptations of an extra-marital affair heard words in his thoughts telling him to sacrifice all for His Lord. For him, they were fighting words—a challenge to make the right choice and a challenge to find the strength to stay on the straight and narrow path. Once while preparing for an important presentation, I realized I had not spent the time to bring myself into the frame of mind to address my large group of employees, volunteers, and friends. With no time to prepare, I simply asked the Lord to prepare me. In minutes, I was humming the John Denver tune, Annie's Song which speaks to an infilling of love.

The Holy Spirit had brought to me the words to lift my soul and inspire me and to fill my senses with His sweet Spirit. The meeting, as always, was a wonderful event full of re-dedicating to our work. In such an unexpected way, the Holy Spirit used the words of John Denver to bring me to a place of heartfelt emotion for the evening that was so important.

Sometimes a poem motivates the weary not to surrender. These words said what a mother needed to hear, "Rest in my timing and work at my pace, all will flow like the earth's rhythms run, as smooth as the tide follows the pull of the moon and sun. (Guided by the Masters Pen, Jane Boston)

The song by Vince Gill, "Go Rest High on That Mountain," comforts a father and son over the suicide death of their wife and mother. Music and poetry can surely carry God's voice to us in our times of need.

Often, Scriptures come alive with new meaning and a verse becomes clearer and more applicable than ever before as it brings to us God's intentions. Many times, we see new answers in a verse read hundreds of times before.

> God gives special blessings to those who are humble but sets himself against those who are proud (1 Pet. 5:5 TLB).

This Scripture helped an employee who had been wronged to be humble rather than angered about being passed over for a promotion. That Scripture gave the worker direction for proper behavior through her challenge.

> Give a warm welcome to any brother who wants to join you, even though his faith is weak. Don't criticize him for having different ideas from yours about what is right and wrong (Rom. 14:1 TLB).

This verse reminded a Christian friend of the need to welcome a new friend despite differences in lifestyles. Scriptures carry God's voice to us. Jesus' parables, Proverbs' wisdom, and the Psalms' praises are there to guide us, inspire us, and reveal Christ's recommendations for life's situations. God can use an open door, a kind word, an inspired lyric, a poem, and of course, His holy Scriptures to communicate His will to us.

God or Coincidence?

How do we know if an act is really of God rather than just a coincidence? Could it be because it meets a need, lifts our heart, brings a feeling of peace, resolves a question, or comforts our searching soul? Certainly. Instances that relate specifically to the matter at hand will bring God's voice to us. Most often, after such an experience, one feels a new confidence and a restored peace to go forward in the direction that has been discovered by the "coincidence."

Mental means of God's communication is another process whereby our mind is the intellectual tool that receives the messages through our dreams, visions, and thoughts. The most difficult part of this means is sorting through our thoughts and Christ's thoughts in us. For me, as you will see in the experiences I relate, Christ's thoughts are what I call perfect. They carry symbolic messages and clever word choices and represent high standards or values. It is a confident thought that has clarity. It is a perfect resolution to your needs—a thought that amazes us as we evaluate our ability to think of the answer we seek.

When I first became the executive director of Hitchcock Rehabilitation Center at age twenty-four, someone said fondly of me, "She was too young her to realize that she couldn't do the job." That was true, but somehow I owned a confidence that whatever was needed of me to perform this job or whatever was needed for the best interest of the facility, I could figure it out. In the early years, my prayers were always for wisdom. Often, people would comment that I was "wise beyond my years." It took me several years and much growth in my spiritual understanding to realize what was happening. I was not getting smarter, as I had originally thought,

Scriptures carry God's voice to us. Jesus' parables, Proverbs' wisdom, and the Psalms' praises are there to guide us, inspire us and reveal Christ's recommendations for life's situations. God can use an open door, a kind word, an inspired lyric, a poem, and of course, His holy Scriptures to bring His will to us.

I was not getting smarter, as I had originally thought, but my thoughts were complemented by the Holy Spirit as I invited His help for my problems and needs.

but my thoughts were complemented by the Holy Spirit as I invited His help for my problems and needs.

Some nights I would go to bed puzzled with a problem or need and arise the next morning with an eagerness to get to work because I knew the exact solution. The real change in my ability to know God's thoughts from mine was when I began to credit Him for the ones that were great thoughts or "perfect" solutions. Over time, I credited Him for small solutions, too, and as you will see, the experiences and clear answers became more and more evident.

Dreams

Most people have dreams that they can remember from time to time. Abraham Lincoln was recorded as dreaming of his death while in office.

The most important reward of all is the peace we maintain within ourselves as we walk away from problems instead of creating them.

"I retired very late. I had been waiting up for important dispatches. I could not have been long in bed when I fell into a slumber, for I was weary. I soon began to dream. There seemed to be a death-like stillness about me. Then I heard subdued sobs, as if a number of people were weeping. I thought I left my bed and wandered downstairs.

"There the silence was broken by the same pitiful sobbing, but the mourners were invisible. I went from room to room. No living person was in sight, but the same mournful sounds of distress met me as I passed along. It was light in all the rooms; every object was familiar to me, but where were all the people who were grieving as if their hearts would break?

"I was puzzled and alarmed. What could be the meaning of all this? Determined to find the cause of a state of things so mysterious and so shocking, I kept on until I arrived in the East Room, which I entered. There I met with a sickening surprise. Before me was a catafalque, on which rested a corpse in funeral vestments. Around it were stationed soldiers who were acting as guard; and there was a throng of people, some gazing mournfully upon the corpse, whose face was covered, others weeping pitifully.

"'Who is dead in the White House?' I demanded of one of the soldiers.

"'The President,' was his answer. 'He was killed by an assassin.'

"Then came a loud burst of grief from the crowd, which awoke me from my dream. I slept no more that night, and although it was only a dream, I have been strangely annoyed by it ever since."

Mr. Lincoln fell silent. The story was over. Ward Hill Lamon looked at the faces in the room. No one spoke. Mrs. Lincoln looked frightened.

"That is horrid," she said. "I wish you had not told it. I am glad I don't believe in dreams, or I should be in terror from this time forth."

The President smiled. "It was only a dream, Mother. Let us say no more about it, and try to forget it."[1]

---

1   Bishop, Jim. *The Day Lincoln Was Shot.* New York and Evanston: Harper & Row, 1955. pp. 55-57

Dreams are fascinating to almost everyone. They happen at a time when our minds are not under the control and restraints of our own conscious thought processes. Our minds are free to flow with the train of thought motivated by our subconscious needs. While many dreams have no particular meaning, those that are associated with God's direction for us are impressive. We remember them as if they just happened. We can see them in our mind like a good, clear movie. Also, we cannot rest with these inspired dreams until we have found the interpretation.

Brian's grandmother, Macie, was deeply concerned about her child's health. She feared for her child's life if the medical condition was not diagnosed. In the night, Macie's deceased mother appeared at the foot of her bed and said, "Your child will be all right." The peace and confidence she desired followed that dream.

Dreams can bring us cautions, reminders of good judgment, and the assurance of God's love. Brian's dream of Scott's angels settled our fears. God is free to work with our thoughts in dreams, as we are not dictating the direction of our thinking. Hearing God's voice helps us serve Him and to know our future paths. In the Old Testament, in Numbers 12:6, God said:

> Hear now my words: If there be a prophet among you, I the Lord will make myself known unto him in a vision, and will speak unto him in a dream.

In the Old Testament, Joseph was made head over the servants of Pharaoh's house because of his ability to interpret dreams. Daniel interpreted the dream of Nebuchadnezzar and was then made a ruler over the whole province of Babylon. Then and now, an inspired dream leaves a strong yearning for interpretation.

Joseph, Jesus' earthly father, also received God's words in dreams. He was reassured of Mary's virgin birth, and he was directed to guide Mary and the infant Jesus into Egypt for their safety. Joseph interpreted these dreams without another man's wisdom. They were clear and to the point. God's communication to Joseph secured the future for Jesus and His family.

Today's spiritual dreams, just like those of biblical days use mental means to relay God's voice. We can usually remember them clearly and are appreciative of God's use of our mind to relay His information to us.

Visions

Visions are much the same as dreams, yet we are awake when they happen. A vision is a snapshot photo, usually a still life, that also has a clear and easy-to-discern message or meaning. The picture usually enters our thoughts unrelated to the current subject on our mind. They are images that can be recalled easily as they leave a powerful impact on our thoughts. Daniel reported visions in the Old Testament. So did Ezekiel, but it was Joel (2:28) who predicted that due to the Holy Spirit, young men would see visions. The New Testament, in Acts 2:17, says: "In the last days, God says, I will pour out my Spirit on all people … and your young men will see visions."

Since the New Testament shows few accounts of visions, we must accept the key words "in the last days." It was not to happen in Old Testament days but rather today. Visions are like dreams, yet we are not asleep. They carry the same desire for interpretation, clarity to recall the scene, and stirring of our soul. They bring

While many dreams have no particular meaning, those that are associated with God's direction for us are impressionable. We remember them as if they just happened.

us warning. They call us to pray for a specific matter. They comfort us. They bring God's voice to us through a picture in our mind. It is easier to claim spiritual ties to visions and dreams because they differ from our regular thoughts.

Abraham Lincoln is known to have had a premonition of his death through a vision. Once the president said he believed that dreams and visions were part of the "workmanship of the Almighty."

> The President said that, before he came to the White House, he was lying on a couch in Springfield and he glanced up at a mirror and saw two images of himself: one glowing bright, one ghastly in death. The meaning, he said, was decipherable: he would be healthful in his first term of office, and death would overtake him in his second. He admitted that, since that day on the couch in 1860, he had tried many times to conjure the same double image and had failed.[2]

Thoughts

Discerning thoughts that are ours from those that are Christ's is probably the toughest call. The Bible helps us with this in its continuous accounts of the ability to gain wisdom through prayer. Wisdom is to be valued but is not a point to be boasted about. Wisdom is desired to help us do right and follow God's will. But we are to give credit for our wisdom to the Holy Spirit, who brings us knowledge.

Paul credits the Holy Spirit for his ability to speak with great wisdom, no longer being a plain preacher without lots of oratory. Matthew 10:20 TLB says:

> You will be given the right words at the right time, for it won't be you doing the talking—it will be the Spirit of your Heavenly Father speaking through you.

Christ's thoughts will be the perfect thoughts ... Solutions that amaze us ... words that come to us that are unlike our own word choices ... efficient, effective solutions.

So how do we know our thoughts are Christ's thoughts in us? Christ's thoughts will be the perfect thoughts. The ideas will be steeped in wisdom, solutions that amaze us, and answers that meet several needs with one step. They are words that come to us that are unlike our own word choices. They are efficient, effective solutions.

Spiritual means are the least understood and are the most clearly questioned forms of God's communication. These involve thoughts that are received with an audible voice quality in our minds, appearances of angels, and the use of the gift of tongues. These require a demonstration of spiritual power to us on earth. Recently, when sharing with a fellow believer of God's acts in my life, she relayed that a friend of hers (an uninformed Christian) was startled by the magnitude of coincidence in a situation. Her response was, "Doesn't that sound spooky?" Yes, it probably does to those who have little or no understanding of the spiritual world around us. We cannot see it in completeness, but through these means, we are given a taste of the inner workings of God's acts that are carried out each day.

I have already relayed the account of the angels Brian saw at Scott's birth. But even today as my understanding of that grows, I believe Brian was allowed to witness the spiritual workings of God's kingdom. Those angels were assigned to

---

2   Bishop, Jim. *The Day Lincoln Was Shot.* New York and Evanston: Harper & Row, 1955. pp. 176-177

those grandmothers, and they came in response to their pleading to save their only grandson. Brian believed it was the picture of actual work, not a "symbolic" photo, long before I came upon that understanding. A new believer might really say, "Isn't that spooky?" But to me it was the comfort, peace, and assurance I needed. I thank the Lord for getting that message to us.

"Spooky" is also a word many believers use when it comes to the concept of speaking in tongues. Truly it is the least understood and most controversial part of God's forms and means of communication. It has truly been easier to ignore this controversial part of the Bible. We have tried to explain the spiritual world in earthly terms. Yet clearly this is all a spiritual matter. Praying is more a moving of the heavens than of the earth. We, as humans, already have the power to do things of this earth; it is the power to understand God that is a skill that needs to be mastered. Though tongues are not the focus of God's communication, it is just one of the many means that can be developed to access the mind of Christ.

Audible Voice

An audible voice in our mind can be a startling experience. It is a voice that stands out clearly as not our own. The words themselves are often grammatically more like the biblical days. Usually, they are words unlike what we normally use.

For example, "You have found favor with God." You find yourself actually thinking, "Where did that come from?" The natural response is to attempt to ignore it, but you can't. Just as an unanswered mystery leaves you pondering, so does the call of the audible voice until you deal with the encounter.

The famous country singer, Billy Ray Cyrus, in the January 1993 edition of *Cosmopolitan Magazine* relayed that he kept hearing a voice say, "Take your guitar and sing." For that reason, he could not walk away from his unsuccessful career in honky tonk. Responding to a message during a Sunday church service at his former small hometown church where his grandfather had preached to him as a child, the minister said, "God wants a desperate man." Shortly thereafter, a major music company cut the record "Achy Breaky Heart," and he became famous. He said, "I will not forget who took me to the dance."

Audible voices are rare and thus loaded with impact to the listener. They can be remembered clearly, just as they were originally heard. How do they happen? Just like all other means of spiritual communication, the soul is stirred, the mind is jolted, and the body responds by hearing. This means of communication is a true spiritual connection. The messages from audible voices are usually related to life's pivotal decisions.

Upon returning to work at the Medical Rehab Center at age thirty after my maternity leave, I was committed to raising the $3.7 million necessary to build the new thirty-seven-thousand-square-foot building. While $2.5 million would be sought through a government loan and South Carolina Republican Senator Strom Thurmond's help, the remaining $1.2 million would have to come through fundraising.

With a new, colicky baby and Brian working fifty hours a week and my assignment being overwhelming, I sat on our couch and said, "Lord, You've got me out too far on this one. I've never backed off from Your expectations of me, but I don't see how all this is possible."

Within minutes, He showed me. I opened my Bible, and my eyes quickly fell upon the Scripture that cleared it up. Exodus 30:36 tells of how Moses raised the money to build the tabernacle. I was to do just what Moses was told to do. I was to

"Doesn't that sound spooky?" Yes, it probably does to those who have little or no understanding of the spiritual world around us.

We, as humans, already have the power to do things of this earth; it is the power to move the hands of God that is a skill that needs to be mastered.

The natural response is to attempt to ignore it, but you can't. Just as an unanswered mystery leaves you pondering, so does the call of the audible voice until you deal with the encounter.

tell everyone of the need, and God would prepare their hearts to give. How about that! Moses was the first fundraiser. A sense of peace came over me. I did believe I could tell people of the need.

Then I received an audible voice in my mind spoken with humor and authority. I heard, "Chill out. This is My thing."

What? I could not and would not have said that to myself. Wow! That was enough. I would rest in Him and let Him proceed.

A year later, the board approved the plan to build the new building. That year, the center received the largest gift we had ever obtained. A $220,000 gift from an estate had been designated in a last will and testament to the center. It was wired to the bank and would be the first deposit that started our building fund. This was just another way of confirming God's voice. This philanthropic act was so perfectly timed and gave great confidence to our plan.

Over the two years we had to raise the money, I told everyone about the need. And in truth, I only directly asked one business for a $20,000 contribution. The deadline was nearing for November 1991. In August 1991, a press conference was held and we presented to the media our need of $700,000 to complete our goal. The treasurer said, "I am confident we will reach our goal." Afterward, he asked me if I was confident we would do that. I expressed to him that I no longer had fear, and it was not my problem or project but God's.

I expressed to him that I no longer had fear, and it was not my problem or project but God's.

The funds were raised. The building was built and opened in October 1992. It was beautiful, functional, and beyond our expectations. More than one thousand people attended the grand opening, and eighteen hundred people toured it the following year. It was an accomplishment so large it could have easily never been conceived except that it was God's will; and that had been demonstrated to me in so many ways during these years.

That same year, I was walking through my home with a laundry basket, and it happened again. I heard a voice. This time the thought was, "You have found favor with God." It was a thought that raced through my mind so fast that I had to stop and stand still to recall it. Pleased, but skeptical, I asked for what I had heard to be reconfirmed. Twice the next day, I would hear the message.

I had learned to walk behind Him and not in front of Him ... to "chill out," and let it be His thing.

A year later, I found in Exodus 33:17 those words given to Moses for his good job. Unbelievable—wow! To hear that and to know that was incredible. I know it was in part for developing my obedience and trusting Him to bring our new building together. I had learned to walk behind Him and not in front of Him ... to "chill out" and let it be His thing.

Audible voices are impact statements meant to help us stay on the path. While audible voices today are less prevalent, angel accounts are surfacing at an amazing rate.

Angels

Angels are described in Hebrews 1:14 as ministering spirits sent to serve those who will inherit salvation. Based on this definition, angels serve the ones who are destined to be saved and who are saved. Angels are workers for the heavens.

Psalm 91:11 tells us that angels are here to guard us in all our ways. In the Bible, angels were most prevalent around Jesus' birth and death and at the end of time. Angels worship Christ. They protect those who inherit salvation, offering help and care for those who are to receive His salvation.

Angels can take on different forms through visions and dreams in our minds or by the unexplained presence of a person or persons in our time of need. More and more accounts today confirm spiritual encounters that involve angels as comforters, protectors, and helpers. Confirmation of angel experiences goes without explanation. The recipients of these experiences are adamant of the life-changing encounters with these spiritual messengers Whether in visions, dreams, or coincidences of helpers, angel experiences are permanently marked on the memory of the human target.

God uses these encounters to convey His presence, love, and protection. Experiences with angels should be widely shared and discussed openly, as these spiritual means of communication that should be cherished. Where angels are concerned, it does appear children can also have connections. With no training or preparation, children are often the ones involved in spiritual encounters.

The birth of our son, Scott, helped me believe that communication between children and angels does occur. It was amazing when, before Scott could talk in complete sentences, I asked him where the angels were. He took me by the hand, went upstairs to his room, and pointed to the ceiling. He was consistent with this for whoever asked him.

At the In Focus Church, members often shared their testimony. One that stood out clearly was the episode involving a child who had fallen from the second-floor balcony of his home the prior week. He landed in the bushes instead of on the concrete. After a visit to the emergency room, there were no injuries. The next morning they asked the two-year-old to take them outside and show them what happened. At the site of the bushes, he immediately said, "Where are the little boys with the wings?" The parents were stunned, yet knew that only the innocence of a child could see the angels at work.

The Gift of Tongues

Speaking in tongues is not so widely discussed and is a point of controversy between many different denominations. The gift of tongues, although a holy gift, has been used by Satan to cause bitter divisions among Christians.

The Bible described this as a *gift* of the Holy Spirit in 1 Corinthians 12-14. The gift of speaking in tongues—the ability to speak in different languages and sometimes unknown phraseology that would otherwise sound like gibberish—has the stated purpose of allowing a person to grow spiritually by communicating with God in a deeply personal way. According to 1 Corinthians 13:1-3, the gift of speaking in tongues is less valuable than core Christian gifts of faith, hope, and love.

The gift of speaking in tongues can be used to instruct or improve you morally and thus build up the spiritual means of communicating within the church. Nonetheless, this gift is an individual gift and is not to be an indication of Pharisee-like superiority over those who may not have the gift. Most Christians, in conservative mainstream denominations have little understanding of this gift. Of the whole Bible, only three chapters in Corinthians are designated to discuss this matter. Tongues were first spoken on the day of Pentecost, a day of miracles and preparation for the coming of the Holy Spirit.

Tongues are described by Paul in 1 Corinthians 14:4 as a tool to help a person grow spiritually. Prophesying, the ability to know God's messages, is more valuable

The gift of tongues, although a holy gift, has been used by Satan to cause bitter divisions among Christians.

because it allows the whole church to grow. Tongues are described as separate from prophesying. Without interpretation, others cannot receive growth or help from the experience … only the person operating in tongues. Paul said that tongues are not a sign for Christians but rather for the nonbelievers. Interpretation is vital because it confirms thoughts so clever, divine, and thought provoking that all who witness it, whether believers or nonbelievers, stand in affirmation that this is an act of the power of God.

Yet, the truth is known that tongues, designed to catch the interest of the unsaved, has become the very part of the spiritual movement that has divided Christian denominations. Paul endorses speaking in tongues privately. Tongues are to be reserved for public display only when we know there will be an interpreter present as well (see 1 Cor. 14:28, TLB).

What if no one is present who can interpret? Then the one who speaks in tongues must not speak out loud. This form of communication is only helpful in open forums if there is interpretation for others who may hear so that the prophetic nature of the utterance may be discerned. With interpretation come knowledge, wisdom, and the power to withstand Satan's attacks. The Bible is clear on one point—the gift of speaking in tongues is not necessarily helpful to others without interpretation (see 1 Cor. 14:5).

The Bible is clear on one point—the gift of speaking in tongues is not necessarily helpful to others without interpretation (see 1 Cor. 14:5).

In other words, it was meant to be a means of communication. If we cannot interpret tongues ourselves or by another, then we have missed the message. The gift of prophecy, preaching messages from God, is recommended as a more effective tool because it brings forth the knowledge of the future. These are delivered in our own language and confirm the two-way communication we need for Christ to direct us.

So, how would one know if there is an interpreter and that God meant one to speak out loud? One would feel it in one's heart and know it in one's soul. The prompting to speak out loud would feel like a burden of obedience. The natural inclination should be to be quiet unless prompted by the Holy Spirit.

Tongues can be spoken silently or quietly in public without distracting others. It is when spoken out loud that Paul believed the condition for interpretation applied. Church services were defined in 1 Corinthians 14:33 by Paul, who tells us God likes order and peace, not disorder. Speakers, singers, and worshippers should take turns. Harmony comes when we, the church members, present our gifts one at a time and in obedience with God's instruction to us in the service. The Holy Spirit will lift us to a level of worship that warms our hearts and renews our energy level to serve Him more.

Paul tells us that there are several different gifts—all valuable and necessary to perform different works in the body of Christ—His church. The gifts of the Holy Spirit are defined in 1 Corinthians 12:28. We are told that each person in the church will be given different gifts. This includes preachers, teachers, prophets who understand God's word, miracle workers, healers, helpers to others, leaders, delegators of work, and communicators of tongues. Based on this, it is clear that we can assume that not everyone should or will receive the gift of tongues. Thus, it would be incorrect to use tongues as the confirmation of the filling of the Holy Spirit or salvation. Paul tells us we have all been given the Holy Spirit upon salvation. God's master plan for most facets of life develops slowly. Flowers start from seeds and develop into a bud; babies crawl before they walk; birds must learn to fly.

These processes are a gradual, step-by-step, and part of maturing. The Holy Spirit enters us upon salvation and becomes more evident as we allow Him with each new spiritual experience.

The demonic supporters have had a field day of our controversy on tongues, yet Paul was quite clear, "Forbid not to speak with tongues" (1 Cor. 14:39). In other words, do not forbid this. As Christians, we have wanted to pick and choose Scriptures, yet the Bible is God's perfect Word. Different people have different gifts and uses. All the talents used together build a body of worshippers fully prepared to carry out the task of Christ's plans on earth. Denominations were not meant to take a stand on tongues. Why? Because they are a personal relationship matter and not a salvation matter. For years, mainline Christian churches ignored or denied the tongues issue. So why is it surfacing today? Because, as we were promised, the power of the Holy Spirit is being poured out at the end of times, and more people today are using the Holy Spirit to build a personal relationship with Christ.

Nondenominational ministries are multiplying at a rapid rate. Their focus is to care for the needs of the flock while empowering people to explore their personal journey with the Holy Spirit. This is an awakening, spiritually, for a generation hungry to understand just exactly what the Bible meant when it promised answers to our prayers.

Tongues are meant to be intimate level of communication with Christ. It requires full submission of our body, mind, and soul. It brings the energy of the power of the Holy Spirit to us. It is undeniably spiritual when witnessed.

Paul said that no gift is greater than love. Love comforts the crying child, gives the aged the will to go on, and gives your spouse the confidence he needs to accomplish his goals. Love never fails.

When we argue over the matter of tongues by tearing down those with the gift or judging those without it we fail at the greatest gift of all, which is *love*.

Tongues are meant to be a personal journey, the most intimate level at which we can communicate with Christ. It requires full submission of our body, mind, and soul.

When we argue over the matter of tongues by tearing down those with the gift or judging those without the gifts of tongues, we fail at the greatest gift of all, which is love.

The Holy Spirit Will be Your Guide

These many means of communication are vital from our earthly position to know and do God's will. It is important to know all the means by which God's communication approaches us. According to 1 Corinthians 13:12 TLB:

> In the same way, we can see and understand only a little about God now, as if we were peering at His reflection in a poor mirror; but someday we are going to see Him in His completeness, face to face. Now all that I know is hazy and blurred, but then I will see everything clearly, just as clearly as God sees into my heart right now.

Just as all people are different, so are the ways God reveals Himself to us. For me, to know more of what God is thinking is a remarkable challenge that I strive to grow in. Through the experiences of others and my own, I do believe that everyone can expand their horizons on earth as they grow in unison with Christ. The Holy Spirit will be your guide. All you must do is ask and believe, and your daily communications will clarify themselves to a point of greater service. As I now relate to you some of my most memorable situations when I heard God's voice, I do so with intent of seeing others validate their own experiences of Christ's voice.

REVIEW & INTROSPECTION

CHAPTER 8: RECOGNIZING HIS VOICE

WEEK

8

1. List below the five methods of communication cited within the text that Christ uses to speak to His people. Give examples of each.

    _____

    _____

2. Of the five methods of communication, which do you experience most often in your personal relationship with Christ? Explain.

    _____

    _____

3. Re-read Abraham Lincoln's accounts of the dream and vision of his future death. How does this make Christ more real to you?

    _____

    _____

4. According to the text, how do we know when our thoughts are Christ's thoughts in us?

    _____

    _____

5. Billy Ray Cyrus reported that he heard a voice saying, "Take your guitar and sing." His obedience led to an unexplainable success. Has God spoken something to you that could lead to your success if you were obedient? Explain.

    _____

    _____

6. In your opinion, what factors contributed to the success of raising $1.2 million for the Medical Rehabilitation Center?

    _____

    _____

7. How comfortable are you with "letting go and letting God"? Why or why not?

    _____

    _____

8. List four learning points about the gift of tongues, and provide their scriptural references.

_____

_____

Scripture References: *What do these Scriptures mean to you personally?*
First Peter 5:5

_____

Romans 14:1

_____

First Corinthians 12:14

_____

First Corinthians 13:12

_____

GROWING IN CLARITY

Who is the Holy Spirit?

How do we know when we receive a message? How do we interpret unusual experiences? How can we be sure they are the real thing? There are several tests for knowing the clarity of God's voice. The Bible describes the Holy Spirit as His messenger. Romans 8:26 ESV says:

> Also, the Spirit helps us with our weakness. We do not know how to pray, as we should. But the spirit Himself speaks to God for us, even begs God for us with deep feelings that words cannot explain.

He is the Deliverer of knowledge, the "worker bee" of the Trinity. The Trinity is a team made up of God, the Planner and Decision maker; Jesus, the Savior and Counselor; and the Holy Spirit, the Messenger and Comforter. Hand in hand, Spirit to Spirit, they perform their work, being respectful of each other's role. So, we must get to know all parts and each player in the Trinity in order to experience God.

The Bible tells us in John 16:12–16 that Jesus could not explain the Holy Spirit to the disciples. He implied we must experience the Holy Spirit to understand.

Over and over, the New Testament reveals to us the Holy Spirit who is a Messenger. He is one who comforts us, one who knows the future, and one who teaches us. He is a Spirit that connects our spirit with God the Father. To accept Jesus Christ as Savior and then to ignore the Holy Spirit makes us useless as a worker to the Father, for it is the Holy Spirit who brings us our assignment. How does He do this? Through the means described earlier. How do we clarify God's voice? By learning how to know and understand the power of the Holy Spirit.

I believe these words were given to me by the Holy Spirit in preparation for this chapter to describe how we treat or mistreat Him:

> Thou art the Holy Spirit, masked by man's emotions, the realm of our inner spirit, the body of Jesus carried to our thoughts. We have overlooked you, ignored you, and denied you and yet you are now ready to reveal yourself to us clearly, calmly, and warmly. You have walked silently beside us long enough. It is time to let you pave the way with the light of knowledge in front. Would a sheep guide the shepherd? Would a baby bird teach the mother to fly? No, it is now time for Me, the Holy Spirit, to take you by the hand and go first, not last, not partners, for I can lead you to the large doors that open to the mind of Christ. These doors are too heavy and too far away for you to move without me. But I will open the doors to your future so that I may shine a light on your path and be a guide unto your feet.

Why is it so hard to come to grips with this understanding? Why didn't Christ make it easier and clearer to hear His voice? Well, for one thing we are told that

Thought of the Week:
We are His servants. How can a servant work without hearing his daily instruction from his master?

Holy Spirit is a Messenger ... who comforts us ... who knows the future ... who teaches us ... a Spirit that connects our spirit with God the Father.

God's direct voice is so powerful that Moses glowed when he came down from the mountain after receiving the Ten Commandments. People could not look upon him but had to turn their backs. The power of a direct account is too overwhelming for humans to handle. Jesus could not explain about the Holy Spirit to the disciples because they would not understand. It is an art. Teaching someone to paint watercolor must be an experience. Reading a book on painting will be useful, but to become an expert, one must convert the knowledge learned into the process of painting.

I am now convinced that the preachers of my childhood were not withholding information on the Holy Spirit, but rather, they simply did not understand what we do today. My grandmother, a saint of a woman, most likely thought of the Holy Spirit as another name for Jesus and God. The power of the Holy Spirit is to be poured out at the end of time (see Acts 1:8).

Are we at the end of time? I don't know that. We are told that He will come as a thief in the night. But I do know that we are closer today than our grandparents were. With this in mind, we should try to gain all the knowledge and strength we possibly can through the Holy Spirit.

During the 1950s, churchgoers sang, "He lives, He lives, written by Alfred H. Ackley." Singers sang about God's ability to talk to them in their daily walk. Christians were singing about concepts they could not explain in the pulpit. As new generations grasped new concepts, most of the understanding of the Bible was not passed down from one generation to the next. This understanding is being acquired today for the first time through inspired pastors who are accessing the Holy Spirit to gain new insights into the Scriptures and through prayerful thought.

Discerning God's Voice

Clarifying God's voice is desired, yet is still hard to understand for us now, as it was hundreds of years ago, as Christ told His disciples in John 16:7 TLB:

> But I tell you the truth, it is better for you that I go away. When I go away, I will send the Helper to you. If I do not go away, the Helper will not come ... I have many more things to say to you, but they are too much for you now. But when the Spirit of truth comes, he will lead you into all truth ...

Communication, both its speed and accuracy, is something we see improving at an amazing pace today. While we open up avenues for email, faxes, and wireless telephones, Christ built a communication system from heaven to earth that is wireless, paperless, and costless. His mind transfers thoughts to our mind through the Holy Spirit's power, His Spirit to our spirit.

Doesn't everyone want to know what God is thinking about the questions concerning our life? Most people do, and yet they lack the knowledge about how to acquire this revelation. Most people have had an occasion in their life during a thought or an experience that was so unusual that they questioned whether it was God's direction. The difference is that some have knowledge about how to discern God's voice.

Most processes in life have phases. So does the clarifying of God's voice. The five phases usually follow this path:

While we open up avenues for email, faxes, and wireless telephones, Christ built a communication system from heaven to earth that is wireless, paperless, and costless.

1. No acceptance of God's voice. You believe prayer is a one-way communication process and that any involvement with spiritual matters is based on moral practices.
2. Acceptance that God's voice can be heard indirectly through human delivery—Scriptures, music, or poems.
3. Acceptance that God's voice can be heard or felt by another person (i.e., a priest, pastor, or mature Christian). You believe it is real for someone else.
4. Acceptance that God's voice can be felt in your heart by reading your emotions to interpret God's directions.
5. Acceptance that God's voice can become a two-way communication process involving you.

What controls how far and how fast one travels through the phases of clarifying God's voice? I believe it starts with a desire and the faith to believe and is complemented with experience and grasping the concepts of the means. It is made more rapid by the testimonies and personal sharing by God's more mature Christians. As a result of others' shared personal accounts, younger Christians move forward faster in their own personal journey.

Physical Confirmations

The signs and evidence of God's voice usually come with three types of confirmations. Physical confirmations are the easiest to discern. They may include a rush of chills through your entire body, or in just one part of the body, such as the arms or neck. Most often this is called "goose bumps." Others experience temperature fluctuations, a rise in body heat with actual skin sensations that are warm to the touch, tingling, lightness in the chest area, a single tear in the corner of one eye, feelings of a cool breeze, a rush of energy, a racing heart, or rapid breathing. Any one or a combination of these sensations may be a physical prompting by the Holy Spirit to listen for God's voice. Just as everyone was made with a special uniqueness, so each person's physical symptoms of the Holy Spirit differ. When they occur, they are promptings from the Holy Spirit to search the thought, question the moment, and seek the message. These physical signs are actually the Holy Spirit claiming His thoughts and acts within us.

When they occur, they are promptings from the Holy Spirit to search the thought, question the moment, and seek the message. These physical signs are actually the Holy Spirit claiming His thoughts and acts within us.

Mental Confirmations

With mental confirmations, we are amazed at the thought. The message, if it came as a thought or an interpretation of a dream or a vision, can often be recalled with clarity in our mind. Often, these confirmations can be discerned as they come to us spoken in a thought. They usually come in word choices that are not similar to your own thoughts but are often biblical in nature or unique in text. The message is clever, creative, and succinct, as is the Messenger. The Messenger does not waste words. Sometimes they are so clever that it may take another believer to help us learn to discern. They may have dual meanings and may tie several thoughts or needs together. Often, once they are heard, they play in our head over and over like a recording on our heart. Or the thought may feel like a deep impression, rather than just words. This could be a feeling of excitement or a burden that directs us to God's plan.

Mental confirmations usually come in word choices that are not similar to your own thoughts but are often biblical in nature or unique in text.

Emotional Confirmations

Emotional confirmations include an overwhelming sense of peace, feelings of radiant joy, and the pleasure that comes from a perfect solution or an exact understanding of a solution. One may describe it as, "My spirit leaped," or a burst of emotion. We may receive a heightened sense of pleasure, peace, and fulfillment. There is often a feeling of relief or release that the work has been done or will be done soon. We are then dismissed from the prayer assignment as we experience fulfillment of the request. We feel an almost uncontrollable desire to share the experience with someone who can confirm that the encounter was real, was consistent with God's ways, and was remarkable and perfect.

The Holy Spirit Will Confirm

How do we grow in clarity? First we must desire to hear God's voice, believe that He can and will communicate with us, and admit He has spoken to us whenever there is reason to believe He has. For by first admitting that He has spoken, He is then free, with your permission, to become louder and clearer upon each need or encounter. The more we confess these encounters before man, the more favor we receive in hearing God's voice. As you can see in my experiences, God's voice became clearer and more frequent as I credited Him for His messages.

Just as preachers everywhere preach, it all actually begins by building a personal relationship with Jesus Christ. He saves us, He opens the door to heaven for us, but it is the Holy Spirit who opens up the line of communication for us. If you are unsure that your message is a message from God, 1 John 4:1–2 tells us to test it by asking the Holy Spirit to confirm it. Another key question is does it go against His Word? Do not feel weak in needing reassurances, as God admires your heart's desires to only believe the truth. On many matters, I wait for three confirmations to support the direction.

God is not saddened by our doubt. He takes pleasure in our patience to be assured we have heard Him clearly. He then knows our desires are to do only what He directs. We are demonstrating our trust in Him when we believe He knows what is best for us. We are demonstrating our willingness to give up control over the decision-making. Finally, we are growing in our listening skills and are waiting and watching for more confirmations.

Most people would admit that God the Father knows our needs and thus, also knows what is best for us, even better than we ourselves can know. From His global view, He can best gauge the path of happiness for our lives. So, the key is learning to receive His thoughts on these matters. The Bible tells us in Romans 8:26–28 TLB:

> The Holy Spirit helps us with our daily problems and in our praying. For we don't even know what we should pray for, but the Holy Spirit prays for us with such feeling that it cannot be expressed in words. And the Father who knows all our hearts knows, or course, what the Spirit is saying as He pleads for us in harmony with God's own will. And we know that all that happens to us is working for our good if we love God and are fitting into His plan.

One may describe [an emotional confirmation] as, "My spirit leaped," or a burst of emotion. We may receive a heightened sense of pleasure, peace, and fulfillment.

If you are unsure that your message is a message from God, 1 John 4:1–2 tells us to test it by asking the Holy Spirit to confirm it.

God's voice becomes clear when we are operating hand in hand with the Holy Spirit. Then we grow to understand His power, know His messages when they come, and use them for the purposes the Holy Spirit intended.

Help!

We are told in Romans 8:26, "The Holy Spirit prays for us when we don't even know how to pray." How does this happen? We spark the energy and power of the Holy Spirit with one simple request, "Help!" Once the Holy Spirit is in us, after we have accepted Christ as our Savior, His power begins to grow within us, but only as much as we let it. We can either maintain total control of our future decision, retain partial control, or relinquish control. The more we relinquish the control of our destiny to God, the more we allow the Holy Spirit to work for us.

I think of this concept again in the sense of delegation. Master delegation was what Christ had in mind—freeing ourselves up and opening up our thinking to let the Holy Spirit direct us.

What does the Holy Spirit direct us to? God's perfect will for our lives! The Holy Spirit can pray for us when we don't even know what to say.

Another use of the Holy Spirit is offered in Mark 13:11. In trials, the Holy Spirit will tell us what to say. And Paul spoke of his increased oratorical skills when the Holy Spirit was in him.

The Holy Spirit is a Spirit, Messenger, and Communicator. He brings Christ's thoughts to our thoughts. When speaking or writing with the help of the Holy Spirit, we are inspired, wise, interesting, and clever. The more we allow Him to work for us, the more He can help. The poor delegator gets little help from the worker, who is not set free to do the job he is assigned. Likewise, the man who does not lean on the Holy Spirit to teach him, advise him, and guide him stifles the Spirit.

Likewise, the man who does not lean on the Holy Spirit to teach him and, advise him and guide him stifles the Spirit.

Achieving Clarity in Prayer

What does His voice sound like, you ask? The answer is many different things. Again, as a reminder, it sounds like Scriptures, poems, songs, dreams, visions, thoughts, or other people's words. It sounds like whatever means God wants to use to send the news.

Just as in a conversation, we must converse. In advanced states of prayer, we are actually able to hold what feels like a conversation. We ask a question. We wait for a person to answer.

One Sunday morning, while in a worship service, my heart was in full worship and praise to my heavenly Father, and I was thanking Him for all He had done for me. I sat and thought, "Lord, how do I tell you how much love I feel in my heart?" Then in my prayer, I said, "Lord, just feel the love in my heart and know it is for You." Then I received this thought from the Father, "I do feel your love, for it is I who filled your heart with that love through the Holy Spirit."

For most people, prayer time is considered a one-sided recitation. We speak, whether verbal or mental, with no pauses, no breaks, and no quiet moments to listen.

Consider your last prayer time. Now think of having your best friend over to share, yet you do all the talking—no break, no pauses, and no room for her advice or comments. She would leave. You have expressed a lot and perhaps feel some greater peace from venting your request, concern, or thankfulness. She leaves

What does His voice sound like, you ask?... Again, as a reminder, it sounds like Scriptures, poems, songs, dreams, visions, thoughts, other people's words.

feeling that she was no help at all because her thoughts were not allowed to be heard, nor were her ideas requested. She was hoping to share, too.

What if we were the one listening when we knew we had the solution, the Comfort, or the answer? So sits God the Father—talked at, not conversed with.

As one advances in this art, prayer time will feel more like conversations. Our prayer time will be a time when our thoughts are relayed and His thoughts are received. Slowly, just as a child builds language skills, so do we grow in prayer skills as we refine the art of listening.

There is usually one component of conversation that makes the difference in shared discussion. That one word is "silence." Great conversationalists know how to ask questions and wait. As a social worker for several years, I relayed without silence and received no information back from my clients. It was hard at first to sit still during "dead air" time. Like most people, I felt compelled to keep talking, so others would feel more comfortable. Yet, in talking, no one was sharing and I missed the message, the problem, the needs, and the assignments. In time, I realized that most everyone could be brought to share if I let them. I then began to understand that if I, a naturally quiet person, was talking too much, then this must be a most common mistake.

This is also the case in prayer. Silence is a priceless, underrated, overlooked component of communication. Why? Because it takes more time to talk and then be silent. Counselors through the years have pointed out how people who are troubled with themselves are afraid to be alone to face themselves. Also, quiet seems boring, and we are all very, very busy.

The Lord has important things to say. Silence is not just golden; it is priceless. As we search our thoughts to know the mind of Christ, we must allow Him to place in our brain the very answer, comfort, or assignments that enrich our earthly days.

Why do God's people find it so hard to hear His voice? It isn't supposed to be this hard, but the devil has made a field day out of "busy"—too busy to listen, too busy to stop, too busy to be quiet. "Be still and know that I am God" (Ps. 46:10). This verse was not a simple comment; it was the answer to hearing His voice.

In my earliest social work interviews, someone could have said to me, "Will you just be quiet so I can tell you what I need from you?" My clients were always kinder than that, because they could see my heart was interested in helping and they were patient. They were often not the ones who were uncomfortable with me; I was uncomfortable with them. I overcame this by experience by talking less and listening more.

That's it. That's how prayer is meant to be. Advanced prayers have held what feels like entire conversations during moments with the Lord.

Ask and You Shall Receive ... in His Perfect Timing

What do people do if they do not hear God's voice? They should continue asking God to talk to them. Debbie, my prayer sister for years, had assisted me in this art, so much that it didn't even seem true that she had not actually heard God's voice herself. Our prayers were more like she prayed and I knew. We were a team.

Then, one day in a time of critical need, Debbie called out to the Lord. While driving, she turned down the radio and waited through ten lonely minutes of silence. Then it happened. In her mind, the Lord said, "It is always darkest before

So sits God the Father—talked at, not conversed with. As one advances in this art, prayer time will feel more like conversations.

Silence is a priceless, underrated, overlooked component of communication.

Why do God's people find it so hard to hear His voice? ... The devil has made a field day out of "busy"— too busy to listen, too busy to stop, too busy to be quiet.

the dawn of a new day." Debbie had been praying for the Lord to come through on a stressful work situation. When she heard this, she knew it was God's own words of comfort.

Why had God not spoken to Debbie before? A friend of Debbie's revealed the answer. Debbie had not heard because she had not asked. Prior to Debbie's experience, I had thought it was lack of faith that silences this communication, yet I now believe it is often because we have not asked with full expectation. The Bible tells us in the Scriptures, "But I know, that even now, whatsoever thou will ask of God, God will give it thee" (John 11:22). The implied idea here is that we have not heard because we have not asked. The Bible also tells us that with the faith of a mustard seed, we can move a mountain (Matt. 17:20). With an even smaller level of faith, we can hear our Master's instructions.

Not all prayer requests are answered immediately. Even for the most experienced communicators, God relays news in His perfect time. At a time of stress, I begged the Lord to take this something from me now. In time, I felt a great sense of immediate knowledge that it was done—He had removed the burden. So why did it take months? Later I understood why. It was because my faith was weak. As the unpleasant matters dragged on, the Lord continued to send me communications, comfort, and assurance He was there for me. Many times when I felt pained and burdened, seconds later I would hear the words, "Jesus loves you, and that is all you need to know." He was not ready to reveal to me the date and time and terms of the end of the matter. He had a greater plan.

On Thanksgiving 1996, my brother Jeff had the most devastating news of his life. After unexplainable weakness and several other symptoms, the diagnosis was finally revealed. Jeff had Hodgkin's disease. At age thirty-three, he was not prepared to face the end of his life. He was told that he appeared to be in phase three of four possible levels, and he was uncertain of what the future would hold. Quickly, he was advised that this is one of the most curable of all cancers and that, statistically speaking, he could hope for a good report and news that he was cured. The news was life-halting for him as he prepared to face the six painful months of chemotherapy. Our family had never dealt with a trauma among the children. We were ready to pray for the miracle of successful treatment and remission that was so greatly desired by Jeff and his family.

A couple of days later, as I was riding by myself, I asked the Lord to tell me what to expect for Jeff. Then I heard these words, "Lo, I am with you always, even to the end." That was not what I wanted to hear. My tears began to flow. In my deep concern, I told my friend Shirley what had transpired. She helped me come to a clearer understanding of this message: "Until the end of the healing." At that moment, I fully accepted that the Lord's will was to bring a full and complete recovery to Jeff. This would be a miracle of life that would bind Jeff to his Maker and Healer and life blood as nothing else could.

As a young person, Jeff had always seemed to connect so amazingly with his Lord; through, this the Lord would allow His love and power to flow through our lives. From that point on, I spent my prayer time thanking the Lord for His love in sparing Jeff and claiming him as such a special person. Jeff has always been such a goodhearted person, who, throughout his whole life, has probably harmed no one. The day of the good report came with chemo complete and the desired medical

I had thought it was lack of faith that silences this communication, yet I now believe it is often because we have not asked with full expectation.

results achieved. God continued to give Jeff the strength to fight when it seemed all strength was gone.

When we cannot hear the complete answer, we can always count on His voice to continue to bring messages of comfort. If it were easy to hear His voice, there would be no effort put into getting to know Him, loving Him, and seeking Him. Over the years, I have come to believe God does love hard work. We all can appreciate the pleasure that comes from successes that are hard earned. If it were easy to win an Olympic medal, we all would have one, and thus, the rewards would not be as significant.

Perfecting the Art of Hearing

Christians who seek a relationship with Christ are like athletes. We must never be satisfied with the quality and quantity of our performance. The Holy Spirit is there to help us with our quest. As I watched my son's own inquiring mind, I realized without his quest for answers, he would lack the knowledge to understand. Questions such as, "What is under my skin?" or "Where does this sewer hole go?" take energy to push until he gets an answer. The Holy Spirit motivates in us the desire to grow spiritually.

Though, personally, I have never been a terribly curious person, the thought of having the power to understand the hand of God has been a quest I cannot back down from. I did not want the Bible to be a book of fairy tales or past history. I wanted the action the New Testament talks about. You must, too.

To hear God's voice clearly and frequently is a quest that should never end. Just as the athlete gets faster and faster at running the mile, so does the Christian at hearing from God. Today, as I seek to perfect this art, I can honestly convey that I find myself more surprised when I don't get a response than when I do. I expect it. I desire it. I acknowledge it to others when I receive His directions. The two-way communication becomes more like a conversation than a recitation.

In Psalms, David says, "My heart heard you say, come and talk with me, oh my people." And my heart responds, "Lord, I am coming" (Ps. 27:8 NLT). David, through the trials of war and hunger of his day, knew he could hear God's voice. All the Psalms convey the belief that God does and will hear us and respond to us. Even before the Holy Spirit arrived on the earth, David, a chosen prophet, figured out how to communicate with God. David was chosen by God to be a prophet and to receive messages from Him.

The Good News is that thanks to Jesus' death and resurrection, the Holy Spirit, who now takes the place of Jesus on earth, allows all of us to open the door for two-way communication.

Salvation is, by belief in Jesus Christ as Savior, asking Him to come into our lives, and it is the only key to heaven's gate. It is our service that paves the road to our assured place with God. We are His servants. How can a servant work without hearing his daily instruction from his master? Clarifying His voice is the path to fulfilling our missions, taking down our assignments, finding our joy, and resting in His peace. In order to clarify His voice, we must live God's way. We must refine our prayerful communication with the Father, and we must desire His will for our lives. We must believe and ask with full expectation. Applying these practices to our lives is the key to refining the art of hearing God's voice.

If it were easy to hear His voice, there would be no effort put into getting to know Him, loving Him, and seeking Him.

I did not want the Bible to be a book of fairy tales or past history. I wanted the action the New Testament talks about. You must, too.

REVIEW & INTROSPECTION

CHAPTER 9: GROWING IN CLARITY

WEEK
9

1. List below the members that make up the Holy Trinity and describe each of their roles.

   _____

   _____

2. According to the text, what are the five phases in clarifying God's voice?

   _____

   _____

3. The signs and evidence of God's voice usually come with three types of confirmation. List them below and describe each type.

   _____

   _____

4. Match the following examples of evidences with their confirmation type.

   1–Physical Confirmations   2– Mental Confirmations   3–Emotional Confirmations
   - a.   Amazing thoughts   ____
   - b.   Goose bumps   ____
   - c.   Heightened sense of pleasure   ____
   - d.   A deep impression   ____
   - e.   Temperature change   ____
   - f.   Uncontrollable desire to share   ____

5. Have you ever felt confused about whether you heard God correctly? How did you handle it?

   _____

   _____

6. According to the text, what major role does the Holy Spirit play in our communication with God?

   _____

   _____

7. Consider your last prayer time. Was it a two-way communication with God—listening and speaking—or did you only speak to Him?

   _____

   _____

Bonus:
Learning to hear God's voice is a process that takes time and effort. Write a short prayer below asking God to make this process clearer and easier for you. Tell Him how much you want to hear and understand His will for your life.

8. *Silence is not just golden. It is priceless.* With respect to our communication with God, why do you think this is true?

_____

_____

Scripture References: *What do these Scriptures mean to you personally?*
John 15: 7–12

_____

Psalm 46:10

_____

IV. ACTING IN HIS PERFECT TIMING

Week 10   Praying Efficiently 87

Week 11   Discerning His Will. 93

PRAYING EFFICIENTLY

Every Thought Is Prayer

God is resourceful in all things. Resourcefulness with our time is valued. Spending time with Christ is necessary to know Him, love Him, and serve Him. Learning to pray efficiently is valuable in accomplishing the most within our limited time.

The thinking here involves two principles: God knows our every thought, and we must have faith to believe He will act, thereby removing the burdens of wasted repetition in our prayers. When we learn to think that every thought is a prayer, we save energy, for God reads brain waves, not just verbal words spoken aloud and eloquently.

God's plan was about efficiency, as we see when we are told Jesus said in John 16:7, "Nevertheless I tell you the truth; It is expedient for you that I go away: for if I go not away, the Comforter will not come unto you; but if I depart, I will send him unto you." The Holy Spirit was to make our work and prayer efficient and effective. Spoken prayers are important. They help move others to the spiritual connection needed to move the hands of God. There is power in numbers. Verbal prayers help train new Christians how and what to pray for.

Verbal prayers please God because not only our thoughts but also our voices praise Him. Our voices call aloud to hear His voice in everything we do.

Be Resourceful in Your Prayer

With every thought being a prayer, God knows our needs. So why must we ask? By asking, we humble ourselves to call upon Him as the provider and to allow Him to free us from the responsibility of handling the problem. Master delegation is a word heard often today in corporate business training. To me, "handle it" is the actual literal master delegation. We delegate by passing the job responsibility on to the most qualified person. Well, that clears it up. Just like an eager worker looks forward to accepting the job assignment for us, so does Christ in taking on our request. He knows He can handle it better, yet we sometimes continue to stand in His way.

Just as a poor delegator wants to step in and tell the eager worker the solution, we try to do this with our prayers. But once we have given the task to someone else, we must trust the eager worker and give him or her room to do the job his or her way. Next, we must thank the worker for a job well done. Master Delegation to our Master works in much the same way. Jesus is the Master and the King of kings. He was sent to walk the earth, save the earth, and be our King. We are called to model Jesus in behavior, actions, and spiritual power. We are called to be kings on earth under His leadership. We have a commanding level of power teamed with humility to be a servant. All this is possible only if our hearts are pure.

For years, I watched unemotional, repetitive prayers from persons praying as a habit rather than with expectations of results. I have always been a results-oriented person. I want results to be fast and efficient. God does too. Jesus wasted no time when He commanded matters to happening. He did not say over and over

Thought of the Week:
Spending time with Christ is necessary to know Him, love Him, and serve Him.

He did not say over and over aloud what He wanted. He prayed succinctly, smartly, and efficiently. He should be our model.

aloud what He wanted. He prayed succinctly, smartly, and efficiently. He should be our model. Confirmation of this practice was demonstrated by God's expectation of Moses when he lost his access to the Promise Land by striking the rock two times rather than once, as he had been instructed (see Num. 20:11).

The thought of us commanding matters into happening scares many Christians because we have been taught to pray for God's will, not our own. As we learn to hear the voice of God, we can pray consistently with His will. Thus, we should pray with intensity and expect God to perform. Though many may be uncomfortable with this, commanding matters into happening is how Jesus, our role model, prayed.

While performing His fist miracle, He did not say, "Father, if it be your will, please, oh pretty please, turn this water into wine." He did not even say, "The water will become wine." He simply told the people present at the wedding what to do. God read the brain waves of Jesus. His words came after the miracle was performed as He told the servants to take some to the master of the ceremonies (see John 2:8). In the raising of the dead, both of the little girl (see Mark 5:4) and Dorcus (see Acts 10), Jesus simply said, "Rise up." Jesus commended the Roman army captain when he asked Jesus to heal his servant, who was close to death. The captain said that it was not necessary for Jesus to come in person but rather to just command the miracle by saying, "Be healed."

Jesus was impressed. This was strong faith and a great example of how to pray. Be efficient, be resourceful, and be direct with your request.

"Handle It"

Until we learn to hear God's voice, we cannot command actions. As we grow, our prayers become more confident. In the Bible, Jesus spoke with few words. He came right to the point. In His sermons, He could draw masses of people. Obviously, He must not have been boring, repetitive, or lifeless in His preaching. Every word He said was a prayer. Christ knows our every thought (see Ps. 94:11).

Once I realized it was not essential that I stop and word things with perfect presentation, I realized I could pray simultaneously while thinking the matter through. "Handle it" has become my favorite way to call upon the Lord. I turn my thoughts to Him and mentally say, "Handle it."

People who know me are amazed at the incredible deals I find when shopping. What is my secret? Again, it is in asking the Lord to guide me. "Isn't it petty to ask God to help on such meaningless matters?" someone might ask. Not when the Lord has asked us to share our life with Him. Wouldn't your best friend like to give you shopping tips? Doesn't God care about our resourcefulness? Yes! My approach is so simple. Between the car and the grocery store door, I look up and say, "Fill my buggy." Before entering the mall, I say, "Let me take home what You would have me buy and let me leave here with what You want me to." Though this is not a perfect science, I can honestly say I am usually amazed myself at the deals I find.

God Supplies All of Our Needs ... Even the Small Ones

Even more amazing is the real story of God's ability to supply our every need. Years ago, during Brian's job change, I realized that all my cosmetic makeup needed to be replenished. Knowing that this would be an expense, I looked up while standing in front of the bathroom mirror and said, "Okay Lord, send the makeup," and laughed to myself. Within a few days, Diane, a colleague and friend, and I planned a trip to

Atlanta for a seminar. It was 1:00 am in downtown Atlanta when we arrived. We drove to the front door of our hotel, and immediately a bellhop appeared to help us. Once in our room, we waited for our luggage and waited … and waited. Finally, the bellhop arrived at our door with the luggage. My second bag was missing, so I approached the bellhop, and he was not surprised when I asked where the missing bag was. The hotel manager had followed the bellhop to my room to explain to me that as they were preparing to bring the bags up to our room, a vagrant swiped my bag when the bellhop had his back turned. They had this on film and would be happy to reimburse me for all the contents.

Amazing! All that was in the bag were bottles of almost-empty makeup containers. The next morning, the hotel manager appeared again with a hundred-dollar bill in hand and directed me across the street to Macy's. If this encounter had not been witnessed by Diane, I think it would have sounded too fictitious to believe. As I mentioned this to a friend, Paul, he said, "It is just like God to use a sinner to reward a saint."

I drove home thinking, *Lord, You have really outdone yourself on this request.* I spent hours on the phone telling friends of this small miracle.

His Perfect Timing

We don't and won't know God's will on certain matters. So often we waste our time trying to tell God the solution. That is not our job. Our job is to give the problem to Him and thus, give the problem up. We surrender the caring of how it turns out. He knows best far beyond what we could plan. "Thank God for unanswered prayers," is a common saying. In many of those cases, we propose the solution to God, but He always knows the best way for us. Only He can see and know what we will have to face.

So often we waste our time trying to tell God the solution. That is not our job. Our job is to give the problem to Him and thus, give the problem up.

We have a fun saying at work that takes the pressure off in times of uncertainty. We say to each other, "I care, but not that much." In this, we let go of what we want and go with the flow. Instead of working against God's will, we surrender. We then stop wasting time and energy wanting what is not meant to be.

Similarly, when it comes to sharing Christ, I only act when God makes it clear that I should. My energy is not wasted and the audience or individual is amazingly ready to receive the information. When we wait for the Lord to direct us, we can score nearly 100 percent in our usefulness of sharing Christ. Instead of turning someone off, we can turn him or her on to the Lord, if we do it in His perfect time. Jesus did not send His disciples to knock on doors. The plan was discipleship: to share with people who cross our path, to gather crowds and teach, to write letters, to minister and encourage church groups, and to be a good Samaritan to our fellow man.

When we wait for the Lord to direct us, we can score nearly 100 percent in our usefulness of sharing Christ. Instead of turning someone off, we can turn him or her on to the Lord, if we do it in His perfect time.

Stay Close to God for a Response

In thinking about how repetitive some of our words are to God, it's humorous to think how boring it must be to hear us. We must sound a little like ministers who can't come to the point or prayers that ask for the same thing worded in fifty different ways.

When my son was four, one night I asked him to pray for someone to get well. The second night when I asked him to pray for that again, he cleared it up for me when he asked, "Jesus didn't hear us last night?" The things we learn from our children are amazing. The faith of a child is what God wants us all to have. Scott said it and meant it. In his mind, it was done in Jesus' name. Our faith, the Bible tells us, relates directly to our ability to command matters into happening. Without a commanding level of faith, we can't make statements like "handle it" and then walk away from the problem.

There are, however, situations when we are called to pray without ceasing. So, how do we know the difference? We pray according to the burden placed on our heart. This is one of the many ways God communicates to us. Someone is in need. We cannot get that person off our mind and our heart. Pray until the burden is gone. Pray each and every time that person comes to mind. Over time, there will be an answer or a sense of closure about the prayer and about the burden. Over time, there will be a clearer feeling of when Christ brought that person to your thoughts. Why? Because as we practice and watch the results, we will learn to know how much prayer God desires on certain matters. We grow sensitive to what God wants and needs from us. The thoughts in our mind and the feedback from our heart help us discern the peace of completing God's call to pray on a matter. Assume confident, commanding faith unless your heart tells you to pray ceaselessly.

While we wait for His answer, it is not like God is trying to make up His mind; He is not in heaven pondering. He knows exactly what the plan is. Stay close to Him to receive as fast a response as He desires to give.

When we pray for a specific need, the number-one question in our mind is usually, "When will God answer?" I have come to think of it like thunder and lightning. When we pray, we can see the lightning as we address the Father. But we hear the answer to our prayer as delayed reaction, just like the thunder, which follows lightning. It comes to us later, yet the two things actually happened at the same time. It is how close the strike is to Earth from the heavens that makes the difference in the speed of the response. The closer we can bring God to Earth near us, the faster the response arrives. In *Timeless Wisdom*, Mother Theresa was known to have said, "Prayer makes your heart bigger, until it is capable of containing the gift of God Himself."

These efficiencies work for me. From my shy background, I grew up knowing you don't have to say much to get the job done. Thus, our prayer time should spend more time praising God and thanking Him for His mercy, grace, and gifts. The typical Christian's emphasis is on prayer for getting what he or she needs. By making that part simple, one can spend more time getting to know God and more time fulfilling His tasks assigned to us.

We pray according to the burden placed on our heart. This is one of the many ways God communicates to us. Someone is in need. We cannot get that person off our mind and our heart. Pray until the burden is gone.

REVIEW & INTROSPECTION

CHAPTER 10: PRAYING EFFICIENTLY

1. According to the text, why is learning to pray efficiently valuable?

   _____

   _____

2. Are the following statements true or false?

   a. T/F _____ God only hears the words you speak aloud to Him.

   b. T/F _____ Because every thought is a prayer, God knows our needs before we even ask.

   c. T/F _____ Prayer is simply talking to God.

3. Define *Master Delegation*. Explain why it is important to incorporate it into your life.

   _____

   _____

4. Revisit Jesus' prayers in Matthew 26:39, 5:9–13 and Luke 23:34. What are three words to describe how Jesus prayed, according to the text?

   _____

   _____

5. Why does the thought of us commanding matters into happening scare many Christians? Does it scare you? (You can be honest here; God knows your heart.)

   _____

   _____

6. "Handle it" is my favorite way to call upon the Lord. What is your favorite short prayer? If you don't have one, take a moment to search your heart for the words that best fit you.

   _____

   _____

7. God provided me with a simple request for new makeup when I needed it most. Do you have a "God supplied my need" testimony? Share it here.

   _____

   _____

8. According to the text, how do we know when to pray and leave the request with God and when to pray without ceasing?

_____

_____

Scripture References: *What does this Scripture mean to you personally?*
John 16:7

_____

DISCERNING HIS WILL

Discerning God's Will

"If it be God's will" follows most dedicated believers' requests. This is appropriate, because we should pray in consistency with His will. But let's challenge that practice one step further.

On most important matters, I want to know what His will is. Applying all the beliefs shared so far, it is consistent with this thinking that we can ask God to tell us His will and He *will*. If you don't think He can tell you His will, He can't, for without the *faith* to believe in two-way communication, we are closed to knowing what His will could be. So those with limited faith to believe that He will share with them must be satisfied to make requests for help without attempting to discern His will.

But you ask, "How exactly will He tell me?" Again, the means of communicating are through body, mind, and soul. They happen through physical, mental, and spiritual means. We are simply, once again, talking about accepting two-way communication. You must believe He can and will tell you. So, here is the twist.

In those cases when God has revealed His will, then we can take the request past "handle it" to actually praying for the solution you believe in your heart He has shared. When the will of God does not match our desires, then comes the challenge.

Kevin's mother was diagnosed with an inoperable brain tumor. He received the understanding that God would take his mother from him; through this he would grow spiritually. This was God's will. Kevin felt an obligation to pray for her healing. He was torn between praying consistently with his belief of God's will or on behalf of his mother's desires. If he cares about efficiency and obedience, he should pray consistent with God's will. Jesus on one occasion prayed a wish that He knew was not the will of God. He asked the Father to, "take the burden off Him," as He faced the upcoming crucifixion. Matthew 26:39 says:

> Oh my Father, if it be possible, let this cup pass from me: nevertheless not as I will, but as Thou wilt.

He knew the plan, but He also knew clearly the upcoming physical pain. Jesus' request was heard, but it was not God's will to remove the cup. If anyone could have changed the will of God, it would have been Jesus. The clear conclusion is that we cannot change God's will.

Everything Is According to His Will

The alternative prayer might be considered a waste of time and a disrespect for God's will. Who are we to think we know better than God what should be done? Only He can see all that the future holds. From His vantage point, it is obvious that His will is best. He wants to say to us, "Trust Me on this one. I will accomplish many things through this sad loss. Later, you will understand and know the benefits."

Thought of the Week:
We are not and will not be perfect at this distant communication. But we are safe with Him when our intentions are pure and our thoughts look to Him for help.

From our vantage point, only in hindsight can we understand what He has in mind. In those times, we can remember Romans 8:28 TLB:

> And we know that all that happens to us is working for our good if we love God and are fitting into His plan.

Yet, usually to most of us God's will is not that clear. Kevin's heart ruled. He continued to pray for a miracle up until her death. God understands. Jesus does, too, as He felt the pain before Kevin. Pray from your heart when in doubt. In the first chapter of James, it says:

> If we want to know what God wants you to do, ask Him, and He will gladly tell you, for He is always ready to give a bountiful supply of wisdom to all who ask Him; He will not resent it. But when you ask Him, be sure that you really expect Him to tell you … If you don't ask with faith, don't expect the Lord to give you any solid answers (James 1:5–7)

We are told over and over by the disciples that God intends to answer our prayers. Matthew 6:8 tells us God knows our need before we even ask it. John 14:13–14 says:

> And whatsoever ye shall ask in my name, that will I do, that the Father may be glorified in the Son. If ye shall ask anything in my name, I will do it.

So, how could we be promised that all our prayers will be answered? It has to do with obedience. As our desires to be in God's perfect obedience grow, so does our nature to pray for only God's will. John's chapters tell us this best. As we seek God's perfect will, we will learn to know this and only desire to pray for what we believe to be God's perfect will, as is described in John 15:7:

If ye abide in me, and my words abide in you, ye shall ask what ye will, and it shall be done unto you.
—John 14:13–14

> If ye abide in me, and my words abide in you, ye shall ask what ye will, and it shall be done unto you.

The idea is that as the Holy Spirit guides us, as Christ abides in our hearts, we surrender our own wishes for the pleasure of obedience to God's commands. At this point, we find ourselves praying for only what is according to God's will, and all prayers are answered in His way and timing. It is then that the power of the Holy Spirit within us carries the will of God forward. Ephesians 3:20 says:

> Now unto him that is able to do exceeding abundantly above all that we ask or think, according to the power that worketh in us.

We then greatly desire the power to ensure us we can assist in carrying out God's will. At this highest point of earthly obedience, we want the things of God only. Should we even want to change the will of God? No. The only account I am aware of where God changed His own will was in the life of Hezekiah. To demonstrate God knows best, He granted his wish not to die. As God extended his life another fifteen years, Hezekiah experienced great loss.

> In Isaiah 39:6, it says: "The time is coming when everything you have— all the treasures stored by your fathers, will be carried off to Babylon. Nothing will be left. And some of your own sons will become slaves. Yes, eunuchs, in the palace of the king of Babylon." At that point Hezekiah said, "All right, whatever the Lord says is good. At least there will be peace during my lifetime." He learned his lesson the hard way.

It is through crises and life challenges that we spiral ahead in understanding His love. We know the hurt of a family for the loss of a child. But many times, if we ask Him, He will tell us why things happen.

It is through crisis and life challenges that we spiral ahead in understanding His love.

But Only If He Chooses …

So, now we must complicate the discerning of God's will by saying this—He will reveal His will, if it is His will to do so. Wait a minute, you say. He said He would tell us if we asked. Yes, but it must be a part of His will for us to know what is to come. In some things, we are actually spared great prolonged grief by plans that are not revealed.

So, how do we know when He will share His will? We must ask Him. If we do not receive an understanding, then that puts it back to the simple format of prayer: "Handle it." But we can be pleased with ourselves that we tried to seek out more knowledge. To me, this step of discerning His will is just like doing homework. We can get an A grade for "handle it." But we get an A+ for actions consistent with God's will. It was an A+ moment for that precious woman who comforted me in the drugstore parking lot. She listened and obeyed the prompting of the Holy Spirit to speak to me. I am sure she didn't know why or how her words of comfort would impact me forever.

Some Prayers Fall Outside of His Will

Some basic criteria apply to limit possibilities of God's will. He would not have His standards for living be breached. In other words, we cannot pray, "Oh Lord, please allow John's wife to leave him and marry me." No. That would not be God's will. The Ten Commandments give us some confines of God's will. Ruling out any requests that don't fit those standards is the starting place for confirming God's will. The request must align with His Word and His will.

Selfish requests that hurt others and only meet our needs are not included in God's will; for example, a prayer that we would win the lottery. When the motive is wealth, it would not be consistent with God's will, remembering He knows our hearts, our motives, and our intentions. Prayers that God help us to cover up an error would likely be out of the perimeter of God's will. For example, "Lord, please help them not to know that the money is missing." This is not something He can join us in. It simply would not be His will. This seems obvious, but we must test our heart before coming to the Lord. God's will for us revolves around one single earthly objective, which is to send people on the path to heaven. We are on a training ground on Earth to prepare to serve God in heaven. It makes us laugh to think that

Selfish requests that hurt others and only meet our needs are not included in God's will … He knows our hearts, our motives, and our intentions.

in heaven we would make a request like, "Please don't let the police officer know that my license tag is expired." God can't join us in these types of requests.

In times of serious need, we have all been known to attempt to bargain with God. We make promises that many times are the reason for the crisis. He didn't intentionally bring the crisis on, but He is certainly resourceful enough to use these instances to move us to a higher level. It was then we prayed to move the hand of God. He heard us, not because we were bargaining, but because we were praying with intensity, humility, and faith. He knew whether or not we would live up to our promise. Nonetheless, the will of God remains unaltered. The bargain had value in motivating a change within us. He was pleased to see the concessions and sacrifices offered. The altering of our heart goes to His attention with pleasure and appreciation, yet God's will stands unaltered. So, why should I bargain? The only good answer is because it may motivate a change for the better, but it doesn't change God's will.

Commanding God's Will

Commanding God's will into happening is a powerful posture. Jesus knew God's will when Lazarus was raised from the dead. Jesus did not raise everyone He saw—just those consistent with God's will.

So, what if we make a mistake in our attempt to command God's will and it turns out not to be God's will? Simple. He loves us for trying to do the A+ level job. God knows our hearts, so He knows our intentions to serve Him at the highest level. He will not be mad at us. He will be pleased that we have stepped out in faith for Him. God's will cannot be altered, but the future on earth can be altered through prayer as we pray God's will into happening.

So, you ask, if we cannot change God's will, then why should we even pray? Because any matter can go in one of two directions—consistent or inconsistent with God's will.

God has allowed Himself to be dependent on our prayer request to bring His will into place. Sure, He has enough power to move the hand of Christ without us, but He chooses not to do so. He wants your support, your involvement, and your assistance. He planned it so that we, mere humans, are responsible for teaming up with Christ to do the work. If we don't pray, He doesn't move. How frustrating it must be for Him! How important it is that He can communicate with us to tell us what to pray for. In other words, God chooses not to implement His will without our support.

Why did God even create man? The sovereign God, the Great I Am, stood solid and confident alone, but it was for the Son that He planned our future in Heaven. It was the work of a Father whose love for the Son would lead to the desire for the Son to have the loving bond of a family, as well as the Father's love. To avoid loneliness for Jesus, He created man to be the eternal companion for His Son.

We, the man, join the body of the church to become the bride of the Lord, as referred to many times throughout the Bible.

> For from the very beginning God decided that those who came to Him—and all along who would—should be like His Son, so that His Son would be the first, with many brothers (Rom. 8:29 TLB).

He wants your support, your involvement, and your assistance. He planned it so that we, mere humans, are responsible for teaming up with Christ to do the work. If we don't pray, He doesn't move.

Why would He bind His own latitude to work without our support? It brings Him great pleasure to work with us, not against us. Just as two colleagues who respect each other's work share greater pleasure completing a project together rather than independently, so does Christ. Working alone is boring. There is no one to appreciate the job, no one to enjoy the discovery, no one to exchange ideas with. He desires to work with us, hand in hand.

He built into man this dependency on God to ensure we got to know each other. Communication skills are essential to a successful job. He knows His will and desires to express it to His children. As in good leadership, it is not the staff's job to question the leader's judgment. But if we must, He can choose to tell us the why of His plans. He can also choose to define nothing more than what should be obvious.

When we can discern the will of God and pray it into happening, it is done in Jesus' name. The task is clear, the plan accepted. The results are achieved. Two-way communication is required to discern His will. It is so pleasing to Him to see us grow in this act. We become efficient and effective prayer warriors as God tells us the plan and we team up with His thoughts to move the hands of God.

Acting Against the Will of God

So what happens when our actions are inconsistent with God's will? He waits. He tries to redirect us when we then choose paths that are not pleasing, not fulfilling, not right for our future. The amazing thing is the freedom of choice He gives us to try to do things His way or to ignore Him and make unilateral decisions.

As parents, we do not give our toddlers the freedom to choose their menu for fear they will only eat cake. To protect them from wrong choices, we as parents intervene. Christ, however, lets us make all of our decisions. Many times, we want desperately to do God's will but can't seem to decide what God wants for us; but we need not worry. If we truly want to do God's will, He will keep us on the path. If we miss the path, He will direct us back to Him. He knows when your heart is for Him, even though your communication skills are too weak to hear His voice. He will guide you if you make God's will your desire.

When He cannot and will not intervene is when we ignore His leadership. He is a God of freedom. He lets us have the room to make wrong judgments, to seek the pleasures of the world, to ignore Him. He waits. He hopes. He capitalizes on crisis. Most of our wrong earthly decisions bring pain, and He knows, if we have ever known Him, we will return. His love will guide us back when we can no longer bear the pain.

An employee named John was promoted to management level. I had no idea at the time he would challenge my spiritual life to a greater level. On an all-day trip in the car, I began to share with him the episodes of my life where I heard God's voice. He was hungry to know more, and I let him lead the conversation by inquiry.

John was raised to know the Lord. As a youth, he loved and lived for Christ. He preached at youth week and knew how to let Christ's love flow through him to others. However, in his twenties, he moved away from his convictions.

Over the next week, I experienced a burden for John's soul like nothing I had ever carried. God wanted him back. He was a jewel in the crown. John knew

It is so pleasing to Him to see us grow in this act. We become efficient and effective prayer warriors as God tells us the plan and we team up with His thoughts to move the hands of God.

He knows when your heart is for Him, even though your communication skills are too weak to hear His voice. He will guide you by sheer fate if you make God's will your desire.

this in his heart but was not ready to give up his lifestyle. Also, John was having unexplainable depression.

He asked me, "Isn't it hypocritical to try to live for Christ while enjoying the bar scene?" I received an answer to John's question, which was, "God says He will take you wherever He can have you."

As I prayed, I continued to feel strongly reassured that God wanted him back. I then found the Scripture upon which this entire book is based,

1 Corinthians 2:16 TLB: "Who would believe we have within us the very thoughts and mind of God, and the power to move the hands of Christ."

I thought about how we all do this. We have loved Him deeply at some points. Then in other periods of our life, we ignore Him, forgetting Him until we need Him to handle a problem that is out of our hands. I realized that in most marriages, this behavior would not be sufficient to keep the relationship healthy. Then I saw something beautiful as I walked up the stairs that night to bed. In my thoughts, I had a vision: Jesus Christ standing over the earth with His arms open wide. These words then followed, "The Savior is waiting to enter your heart. Receive Him and all of your sorrow will end within your heart; He'll abide."

On Monday, after our Friday car trip, I couldn't get to John fast enough to say, "God wants you back. I believe by the end of the week—by midnight Friday—you will receive Him and your depression will end." Throughout the week, we shared. He was trying but unsure he was worthy or ready to go back.

Then it happened. Saturday morning at 12:03 am, while returning from an evening at the bar, he surrendered his resistance and opened his heart to resume his life for the Lord. He laughed. It was easy to agree to go back. Why had it seemed so hard? Then another funny thought—Jane missed it by three minutes. We are not and will not be perfect at this communication. But we are safe with Him when our intentions are pure and we look to Him for help.

REVIEW & INTROSPECTION

CHAPTER 11: DISCERNING HIS WILL

1. Recall the two attributes from chapter 7 that are necessary to hear God's voice. They are also necessary to discern His will.

   Faith   Salvation   Baptism   Fellowship

   Forgiveness   Works   Spiritual Gifts Desire

2. Read Jesus' prayer in Matthew 26:39. Why do you believe He prayed this prayer?

   _____

   _____

3. Will God answer all of our prayers? Yes or no _____.
   Explain how obedience affects our prayer life.

   _____

   _____

4. The text cites four types of prayers that God will not honor when praying for His will. List them here.

   _____

   _____

5. When we fail to do the will of God, what happens, according to the text?

   _____

   _____

   Has God ever had to direct you back to Him when you strayed away from His will? Explain.

   _____

   _____

Scripture References: *What do these Scriptures mean to you personally?*
Matthew 26:39

_____

Romans 8:28–30

_____

James 1:5–7

_____

John 14:13–14

_____

Ephesians 3:20

_____

V. WORKING IN RHYTHM WITH THE MASTER

Week 12   Exciting Assignments........................103

Week 13   Friends in High Places.....................113

EXCITING ASSIGNMENTS

Serving Him is Exciting

Most humans are thrill seekers by nature. "It's boring," is the phrase that comes from the mouths of children restless for action. We need constant stimulation to satisfy our fast-paced appetite for excitement.

Christians are often viewed as dull, boring, conservative individuals who avoid excitement; and that can be the case, if our only goal is to observe Christian moral codes. The real excitement comes for Christians who access and apply the Holy Spirit's power on Earth. Learning and growing in this art is the most exciting thing I've ever encountered. Day after day, I awake wondering what Christ will do with me today. Through certain periods, I rest from these callings because it takes so much energy and initiative to keep pace with Christ's work. When I rest for days or weeks or even months, I can enjoy being a boring, dull, regular earthling because Christ has worked me at such intensity that I can cherish the break. This is not a dull, boring Christian life.

It's the in-filling of the Holy Spirit that keeps churches alive and pastors enthusiastic. The Holy Spirit grows in us. This is God's format for most of life's processes. The Holy Spirit's power in your life is progressive. Just like babies grow into adults and flowers mature from buds to blooms, so the process of growing in the Holy Spirit is one of maturing.

The Holy Spirit enters at acceptance of faith in Jesus, but it is the growth of the Holy Spirit that moves us to service. The Spirit helps us pray even when we do not know what to say (see Eccles. 7:1). Romans 8:26 shows us that the Holy Spirit prays for us with great feelings.

The Holy Spirit is the catalyst for excitement in God's work. God should be our pilot, not our co-pilot. The freer we are to follow God's guidance, the more interesting and exciting is our time spent with the Lord. We are called to serve.

The *In Focus Church* newsletter column by Dr. Gene Smith helps to explain the Spirit-filled believer:

> There are at least two types of Christians—those who are overly influenced by the world and end up wasting their lives while on earth, and those, who by continually being filled with the Spirit, live productive, joy-filled and victorious lives.
>
> What does it mean to be filled with the Holy Spirit? Baptism in the Holy Spirit is a one-time event. The filling of the Holy Spirit is an ongoing process that lasts and grows during the entire lifetime of a believer. Once I understood this principle, it opened amazing new levels of understanding of the Scriptures. The Holy Spirit-filled believer brings their entire existence under the dominion and control of God's Spirit (Dr. Gene M. Smith, *In Focus Church, Augusta, Georgia*).

Thought of the Week:
It's the in-filling of the Holy Spirit that keeps churches alive and pastors enthusiastic.

Submitting to the Holy Spirit

The personal control issue is always in the forefront in your relationship with Jesus Christ. Yet, the more you submit to His will, the wider the world of excitement in serving Him becomes. Scriptures mean more to you under the light of the Holy Spirit. The answers were always there to allow the Holy Spirit to work in you, but just as a person who could not see the forest for the trees, so do we often miss the point concerning how to bring action into our spiritual lives.

I wanted to know what God meant when He said, "All our prayers would be answered," "We can move the hands of God," and "The wages of sin are death." All these words and verses were boring, meaningless, and empty before my submission to allowing the Holy Spirit to work in my life.

The person who wakes up each day to serve has an unusual amount of energy, enthusiasm, and excitement. We all love to experience a plan when it comes together. Watching Christ's plan come together, you will know He is the master of amazing details, and you will never see such masterful planning outside of Him. Often, one plan or action serves several purposes. His work is effective, efficient, and clever.

> Watching Christ's plan come together, you will know He is the master of amazing details, and you will never see such masterful planning outside of Him.

As we grow in service, we grow in every area of our life. Our personalities become more radiant. As I have submitted to Him, He has sent people to mature me. While having a wonderful childhood that was rich in love, Brian has helped me become the person Christ meant for me to be. My work exposed me to impressive mentors. All my needs have truly been met, and usually I have more energy than I know what to do with. My life has been exciting, as I now ponder what could come next. Excitement brings energy, and energy, in turn, brings more excitement.

My down time is usually spent on the telephone with fellow Christians. The first line out of our mouths is, "You won't believe what happened today." It is with great excitement that we share our stories of Christ's hand at work around us.

Surrender to Your Personal Ministry

We mortals are in pursuit of our purpose during this life. Those who find their mission live with joy and don't ever stop searching. Many find life's fulfillment through means not of Christ, but true and perfect joy is reserved for those who live out the role Christ intended.

Matthew 16:27 tells us that it is by Jesus we are saved but by fulfilling our missions we are rewarded. What is the reward? Joy on earth and appreciation in heaven. That is enough. That is all one could or should ever want. "He shall reward every man according to his works" (Acts 20:24 NLT) Paul tells us he lives to finish his course with joy and the ministry for which Christ called him. And he reminds us in Acts 20:24, "But life is worth nothing unless I use it for doing the work assigned me by the Lord Jesus."

> We confuse ourselves into thinking that a call to the pulpit is the only way to minister.

So, if we want joy and peace, why do we often not find our ministry? I believe that we may misunderstand the call. We confuse ourselves into thinking that a call to the pulpit is the only way to minister. That is incorrect. God calls His children to work in all walks and places on Earth. One's mission is to raise his or her children to become responsible adults. Another's mission could be to be a schoolteacher, a banker, or a baseball coach. In all walks of life, we influence people, share successes, and fulfill God's daily assignments.

We focus so often on people who denied their calling to the pulpit until Christ won. These are persons needed for that particular role. No matter where or how we are to serve Him, the key to fulfilling our missions is the surrendering of our own will. That "surrender" word appears again to remind us to give up our own wants and let Christ's will rule.

Christ said it very clearly. Only those who give up their lives will find their lives (Phil. 1:21). Christ showed us the most dramatic surrender on the cross. He showed us that by surrendering our life to Him, we would receive a place in heaven. The surrendering of our own decisions to Him allows us to experience the peace of heaven while on earth. There is joy in living the harmonious life that Christ has prepared for us.

Living God's Plan Is a Choice

It is a choice. God does predetermine a plan, but it is our choice to follow it. He is dependent on us choosing His plan over our own. Why did He give us a choice? Because He knows that a forced plan brings resentment and rebellion. His idea is to let us learn to look to Him and He will, with our permission, bring us to the work that brings joy.

Someone recently said to me I was so lucky to have a job where I could serve my community and my Lord at the same time. This was offered in support, yet my fate was very different than luck. I do not believe I was lucky. I believe I was insightful at a young age to have had the wisdom to believe that to surrender my future to Christ was the right thing to do. In return, I received the joy that comes from living God's plan for me.

Why is it so hard to find that plan God has for us? Usually we are looking too hard. We are born with certain strengths and weaknesses. These generally relate to our calling. It is through the personal relationship with Him that we find the plan.

Barry Given, a twenty-four-year old college baseball coach in Aiken, South Carolina, relayed his story of God's manner of getting his attention. In his story, as reported by Roch Erick Kubatko in the *Arundel County Sun Newspaper*, Barry, a nineteen-year old high school athlete at the time, was one of the finest athletes to come out of Annapolis, Maryland, his hometown. As starting quarterback, the leading scorer on his varsity baseball team, and a good student, Barry had the world in the palm of his hand. That is until one morning when he woke up with total, but undiagnosed paralysis to his left arm and shoulder. Three days later, he still had no movement in his arm. Efforts to raise it in any direction were futile.

> Doctors informed Given he had suffered nerve damage in the shoulder, either from a hit sustained on the football field or from a rare virus that prevented stimulation of the deltoid muscles. Spinal taps were performed. The atrophy in his shoulder would worsen each day. The left arm now hung lifeless at his side. "It started out where my parents had to move it back and forth so the joint didn't freeze up forever," he says.
>
> Broadneck High School baseball coach Mark Stover said, "If you looked at him, it looked like one side was completely disproportionate to the other. I had never heard of something like that happening before or since.

In all walks of life, we influence people, share successes, and fulfill God's daily assignments.

I believe I was insightful at a young age to have had the wisdom to believe that to surrender my future to Christ was the right thing to do. In return, I received the joy that comes from living God's plan for me.

Given says doctors were giving him a one-percent chance of full recovery. Playing baseball—which was his true love in sports, was out of the question (Roch Eric Kubatko—*Arundel County Sun Newspaper*).

Barry rehabilitated with the motivation that only great athletes can muster. Through pain and disappointments, he pressed on. He had an almost complete recovery. The most remarkable point of his recovery was his experience at a healing mass at Our Lady of Victory Catholic Church, under Father Larry Geisy (led by Catholic sisters). As a Catholic, Barry understood Christ's salvation, but it was at this mass that Barry experienced a level of spiritual power never before revealed to him. The Lord brought him emotionally to a level of inner peace that lasted for minutes. It was a life-changing clip of time. At that point, Barry realized the ambitions of this world were no longer of value. The self-focused, celebrity, athletic star role was nothing compared to serving Christ. The traumatic injury had redirected and refocused Barry's life to be Christ-focused rather than self-focused. God had gotten his attention. Barry would never forget the moment. He clearly saw his direction and deepened his commitment to do something for Christ.

Instead of anger over this paralysis, he was, even at that young age, able to see why this had happened. His heightened faith and remarkable stamina to overcome the physical loss led Barry back to sports. Attending college on a baseball scholarship opened the door for him at age twenty-four to be the youngest head baseball coach and assistant coach in the Southern Peach Belt NCAA Division II League. As a coach, Barry focused on sharing team values and rewarding players' unselfish acts—a focus that was a direct result of his desire to obey God's call in his life. I watched Barry display integrity in his personal and professional life. I learned from Barry that even if you don't know how to hear God's voice, He will find you and redirect you if your heart is receptive to the Lord. I was also reminded from Barry that you feel God's voice before you are able to hear it.

> ... even if you don't know how to hear God's voice, He will find you and redirect you, if your heart is receptive to the Lord.

The key thought is in the belief that it is virtually impossible to waver from God's will when He knows the desire of our heart is not to stray from him. It is a heartfelt prayer to Christ when we, in all our blindness, just say, "Lord, send me." Barry had always thought his story would be told and shared somewhere. How about that? A hunch. A spiritual cue. By submitting to Christ, Barry found the door to publish this miracle account.

Find Your Way to Serve Christ

Hearing God's voice culminates in receiving our missions. Whether we hear clearly, directly, or indirectly, we must have some connection with Christ to get our assignments.

Carl, a SWAT team officer in Phoenix, happened to sit next to me on an airplane flight home. It was a chance meeting, as my seat had been reassigned and he almost missed the plane. He began to read a *New Testament Handbook for Peace Officers*, and within seconds, he and I began to share our beliefs. As a law enforcement officer for the Bureau of Alcohol, Tobacco, and Firearms, he had found his own way to serve Christ. It was an amazing application of the power and knowledge of the Holy Spirit. At just thirty-three years of age, Carl and his wife were completely committed to serving the Lord. Carl's colleagues were often amazed at how he solved his cases at work. He did not always understand as he watched the details of a case unfold as the Holy Spirit led him.

Carl's goal was to become completely trained as a peace officer, an accepted approach in many crisis situations. He was prepared with the ability to defuse situations by listening. He knew the emotions of people under stress and could use his insight to calm hostility. He was on this plane traveling to Atlanta for special training to become fully versed in hostage negotiations and expected to help free innocent people from harm, using this skill and his own well-developed ability to access the mind of Christ. Wow! What an application. If Carl could find a Christlike mission as a SWAT team law enforcer, the a Christian in any honorable vocation could. My thoughts were, *If my loved ones are ever in this drama, please ... send Carl.*

Wow! What an application. If Carl, as a SWAT team law enforcer, could find a Christlike mission, then any vocation could.

Some Assignments Require Obedience

The lesson found in Joshua 5:6 tells us that if we do not obey the voice of the Lord, we cannot expect to receive His blessings, just as the Israelites did not enter into the land of milk and honey. But what if the job is something we do not want to do? Well, again the Bible tells us in Philippians 2:13 TLB that Christ is at work within us to help us want to obey Him.

God has called us to obedience. He gave men of the Bible very specific assignments: build an ark; prepare a portable tabernacle; perform specific healings. Today, He desires to give us specific assignments too. We must be watchful and ready to act as called. Abraham, it seems, was challenged to the highest test when asked to sacrifice his son. It was a test of obedience. One has to think that Abraham's communication skills with God were advanced. In Genesis 22:3, we are told of Abraham's intent to be obedient.

Today, He desires to give us specific assignments, too. We must be watchful and ready to act as called.

All Christian work revolves around one objective—to take as many people with you as you can to heaven. Billy Graham accepted this calling completely. Much of our daily work is in relationship building that prepares people to see Christ in us. A great philosopher, Thomas A. Kempis who published The Imitation of Christ, once said, "On the Day of Judgment we shall not be asked what we have read, but what we have done."

All Christian work revolves around one objective—to take as many people with you as you can to heaven.

For many years as a young professional in the field of social work, I accepted that it was my right and station to stand up for wrong, bring patient advocacy issues out, and change those things in society that were unacceptable. I put much energy into this and had good results. Yet, now, I see a new way. Becoming a rebel is not exactly what Jesus advocated. His commandment to us is to turn the other cheek and to do unto others as you would have them do unto you.

So, how do we affect positive change? We pray it into happening. It is a much quieter, calmer, more acceptable way to achieve results. It takes less energy and gives more freedom to let things evolve onto the right track, rather than to force the issues. It is amazing how much more professional it all comes across. We still do have to act, but it is more like a colleague of mine said, "I look at God like, I just do the footwork and He does the rest." When we are not positioned in the role of a rebel, we can stay focused on the results and not on the issue. Simply pray it into happening.

We must hear God's voice to find our mission, yet God usually begins by speaking to and through our hearts before we hear Him in our head. Romans 8:16

TLB says, "For His Holy Spirit speaks to us deep in our hearts, and tells us that we really are God's children."

Pray and wait. It is much easier to do this once we have learned to hear God's voice. Each time we need to wait, He will reassure us of His hand in the matter. Through His voice, we will then find a renewed level of patience with even the most difficult concerns. My pastor said you can tell the man who truly trusts God—he is the one who says, "Okay Lord, I've given You the problem. Now I am going to go to sleep while You work this out." Once you are feeling clear about what steps seem to be exact and right and you feel confirmed in your heart, then you are free to act efficiently and with confidence.

No Excuses—You Are Qualified!

What if the job is something we do not feel qualified to do? Paul explained this in relaying that he used to be a poor orator until the Holy Spirit filled him. Christ will strengthen the areas needed to carry out His work. Proverbs 16:3 ESV tells us, "Commit your work to the Lord and it shall be established." In Philippians 4:13 ESV, Paul said, "I can do all things with Christ in me." There are no good excuses for not doing a known assignment.

Unknown assignments are our greatest failures. Until we can communicate perfectly with God, this will continue. To know Him, to love Him, to serve Him; this should be our aim. By simply telling the Lord you are available, the Lord can position an open door to serve.

Today, the Holy Spirit, through His people, carries out miracles. Today's healings often tie directly into modern medicine. In rehabilitation, people often say they are expecting a miracle. Great! Yet, my fifteen years of experience show that most of God's miracles of healing are natural, slow, and hard-learned by the believer. Today, thousands of people live after cancer. Many amputees walk. Legally deaf people are restored to functional hearing with hearing aids. People pronounced dead return to life with lifesaving equipment. When healing is sudden, radical, and unexplainable, God is often credited. Yet, He is the source of all recovery, and we are His assistants.

Power Brings Influence

Carrying out large-scale, world-changing assignments requires power. As Christians, we have been afraid of the word "power," thinking that power corrupts. But if our hearts are pure, power can be the required tool to do the big jobs. God wants and needs people in all walks of life—housewives and CEOs. I have finally realized that Christ needs Christians who are positioned with earthly power for the big jobs. Why? Because power brings influence. Influence allows many people to be reached. The larger my network of associates, the more help I can be. So where does the fear of power come from? It comes from the fear of obsession with power, loss of humility, and attention to self rather than Christ.

Money, intelligence, energy, and personality can bring power. These are not bad qualities. These are desirable qualities when kept in balance with humility. Great admiration goes to people who can manage these resources wisely. The resources are useful to Christ when properly balanced and used for His glory. When assignments come, these resources can help us to carry out the tasks.

I have found a pattern of how God works with us. He gives us many assignments, and everywhere we turn there may be a person, a project, or a task. Then, in His fatherly wisdom, He gives us rest from assignments. The rest may be long or short, depending on what God wants to accomplish and according to our own needs for rest.

A dear friend, Vivian, came to me to share some concerns she had. A former missionary, she and her husband wanted to return to that level of service. Every door that had ever been opened for this opportunity in the recent past closed. Why wouldn't God accept their offer to full service? In prayer, I received the following thought for Vivian. I believe the Lord said, "Rest in My love. Expect nothing, as I expect nothing of you right now. Be still and feel My favor for you. You are a child of God, eager to serve, yet I call you to grow in trust that I know what is best for you. Your struggles are in vain, for I give you a gift of self-insight during this test of obedience. Your gift to gain will be a rising of your discipline to follow, not lead. Your desire to serve will calm My footsteps as you surrender to My love. I am calling you to one thing only for now—My love. Rest in it."

In time, God has recalled this beautiful couple to full-time ministry. The time of rest, those years in between, were part of what God wanted for them.

Reach Out and Touch Those around You

So, what is the key to fulfilling missions? It is in the offering to do the job. Beginning means are simple. Offer acts of kindness to those around you. Reach out to meet people, even strangers, when you are prompted. Just as the lady reached out to me after Scott's birth in my time of need at the perfect moment, your own initiatives could be the miracle someone else is crying out for. Most of what we need during times of our own crisis is reassurance. If you feel prompted to reach out, do not hesitate to do so. Encourage everyone you meet. People love feedback about themselves. Try to access a sincere, positive virtue of that person and offer it. People are usually shocked.

I recently told an older man he had a nice voice. He literally rose taller in height. Write lots of notes to encourage and remember people. Stay in touch with your friends; they may need you someday.

Jesus told us to start our service with small things in Matthew 25:23:

> Well done, good and faithful servant; thou hast been faithful over a few things, I will make thee ruler over many things; enter thou into the joy of thy Lord.

Once you get past the natural and obvious assignments, Christ will keep moving you to higher levels based on your willingness and desire to serve Him. Stand ready to do things far greater than your own imagination, far easier than under your leadership, far greater than your own natural talents, and far more fulfilling than the things of the world. "Blessed is the man that heareth me, watching daily at my gates, waiting at the posts of my doors" (Prov. 8:34).

Seeking to understand the whys of this spiritual world is a quest I hope never ends. It is with pride I can now sing the hymn, "He Lives, He Lives by Alfred H. Ackley". I know my Lord walks and talks to me as he guides my daily plans. Today I know what those words really mean. I have seen the inner workings of a spiritual world unclear to me as a young person. As people all across America grow in the Holy Spirit's power, the excitement for Christ will expand. Boldness to tell Christians the truth of the power to move God's hands will no longer be silenced in a world hungry for God's voice.

REVIEW & INTROSPECTION

CHAPTER 12: EXCITING ASSIGNMENTS

1. According to the text, what brings excitement into the lives of Christians?

   _____

   _____

2. Re-read Dr. Gene Smith's passage in the *In Focus Church.* At this moment, which type of Christian are you in your Christian walk?

   _____

   _____

3. Why, according to the text, is it important to be excited and energetic in God's work?

   _____

   _____

4. What is cited as the reward for fulfilling our missions as Christians?

   _____

   _____

5. Are these statements true or false?

   a. T/F _____ God has a predetermined plan for your life, but your acceptance of it is a choice.

   b. T/F _____ We are not born with strengths and weaknesses; we develop them over time.

6. Carl, the SWAT team officer, found a way to interweave his faith with his work. How can you use your faith to become more effective at your work?

   _____

   _____

7. 7. All Christian work revolves around one objective. List it here:

   _____

   _____

Bonus: *The man who wakes up each day to serve has an unusual amount of energy, enthusiasm, and excitement.* In a short prayer, commit to serving God every day and trust that He will give you the energy, enthusiasm, and excitement you need to do so!

Scripture References: *What do these Scriptures mean to you personally?*

Ecclesiastes 7:1

_____

Romans 8:26

_____

Acts 20:24

_____

Philippians 1:21

_____

FRIENDS IN HIGH PLACES

Work Closely with the Master

Who do you know? The question comes up in the business world often when we are seeking to strengthen our position on a matter. If you had the ear of the ruler of the Universe, wouldn't it seem that you should use that contact to guide your success? We have friends in high places. We have clout for implementing plans and favor by working closely with the Master. We are told in Proverbs 8:34–35, "Blessed is the man who listens to me, watching daily at my doors, waiting at my doorway. For whoever finds me finds life and receives favor from the Lord."

Just as in the work world, when the Boss knows we will implement the plans to His liking and specifications, our level of responsibilities grows. God stretches our faith with each assignment. Is He using you today? If you are in your comfort zone, you are not where God wants you to be. Faith is a place of confident assurances that something you want to happen will. Faith is the fuel of the spiritual engine. Faith is the beam that carries your prayer to heaven. God keeps us at a place of trust while walking in the unknown.

A seasoned businessman introduced me to a colleague by saying, "Jane has taken incredible risks in her career." I was shocked. It didn't feel like that to me. My level of faith keeps me at peace even through some very large earthly assignments: building a 3.7-million-dollar medical rehab center, starting a new company, operating a 1.2-million-dollar corporation, writing a book about hearing God. I realized while handling large projects that there were so many unknowns, but the intrigue was watching those projects come together as I learned more about God's timing. His timing is impeccable, "coincidental," and perfect. I have learned how to lower my risk by hearing from God on each step.

Knowing When to Wait and When to Act

Knowing when to wait and when to act is always a critical question in implementing a plan. Now that we can see that God's timing is perfect, we must figure out how to find the rhythm to work with Him in perfect unison. Timing is rhythm. There is power in rhythm. In poetry, timing and rhythm raise our emotions. In music, we feel the song when we are moved with the timing of the beat.

During the years when the railroads were built, hard-working men had to move and lay the railroad ties. One man could not do this alone. But as a team, they found when they moved in a rhythm, their timing brought them power far beyond the team's normal strength. They made chants to work by and became known as the Gandy Dancers. They found the power that working in rhythm brings. Rhythm brings emotions, energy, and passion. God's perfect timing feels right to us in the same way. When He calls us for a task, the desire to act brings with it some important reactions in us.

Confidence to act comes with the direction to act. When Joan acted by inviting her niece into her home, despite her limited resources, she received a confidence that she could and would answer the request. Confidence to act is vital when we hear God's

WEEK 13

Thought of the Week:
We have friends in high places. We have clout for implementing plans and favor by working closely with the Master.

actual instructions. When we have waited and received clarity on the matter, it should feel harder *not* to act than to act. The rhythm and timing will feel right, and confusion and doubt will be absent. The more seasoned we are, the more sure we act for Him.

Brian's grandmother, Macie, is a great American story in herself, regarding a woman holding her family together through adversity. At age fifty, her husband left her with four children who ranged from teenagers to a twelve-year-old. Two years later, she had a stroke that left her unable to work. Her eldest son, born with a heart defect, would face several surgeries. The loss of a child at birth earlier in her life and the death of her mother would all be traumas she passed to the Lord for peace. Her eldest son, Wayne, died from his heart-related conditions. He had a life full of stresses, but she knew he was with the Lord. Nonetheless, all of us at the funeral felt her deep sorrow. Without thinking or planning to, I spontaneously leaned over to Macie at the funeral home and said, "God is going to send you a vision of peace." She nodded. We hugged. As I walked away, I was stunned. The confidence to act was so strong, I didn't even evaluate what I was saying.

When we left the funeral, I told Brian, and he agreed we would pray. I felt obligated. She must not be let down in this comfort. During the next week, I received a phone call from Macie. It was the only time in ten years she had ever called me at work. She said, "You know that dream you told me about? I had it, and it brought me peace."

Macie went on to relay that morning as she awoke she recalled all that she had dreamed. Her mother, Wayne, and she were walking on an old dirt road to enjoy a covered dish picnic in the woods. The tables were filled with food, and the day was beautiful. As they left to go home, the rain began, and the dirt road became a stream, which grew into a river. Soon, she was on one side and her mother and Wayne on the other side. Wayne said, "Mama, come on over, swim through to get over here. The desserts are on the other side." Macie, afraid of water, said, "No. I can't come over now." As she awoke, she knew that Wayne was in heaven, accompanied by her mother. The time for her to join them was not here, but the peace the dream brought to her was all she needed to rest in God's love. She knew she could not or would not wish Wayne back to earth. I learned that by acting in God's perfect timing, comfort was brought.

Don't Miss the Assignment

Communing with God must become our way of life and must be two way in our understanding to be able to work in His timing. Prayer is used so freely as a term for asking God. In the book, *Timeless Wisdoms*, Mother Teresa was known to have said, "There are some people, who, in order not to pray use the excuse that life is so hectic that it prevents them from praying. Prayer does not demand that we interrupt our work, but continue to work as if it were a prayer." A child once said, "God sometimes I think about you, even when I am not praying." This is a compliment, since God is measuring the space for Him in our heart and in our day.

What is interesting to realize is that praise to God has the same impact on Him that is has on us. If someone praises us, we are lifted, energized, motivated, and empowered. God wants our praise for that same effect. When we are waiting, praise is a most effective use of our time, as it empowers the heavens to move, maybe even to move for our needs or certainly some other need that God has before Him.

Relinquishing control is vital to be able to move in God's timing and plans. When we do pass the baton to God, He will bring us to a new level of peace as we wait on Him. When we act, we no longer have to worry about results, funding, logistics, and reactions. We are operating as a servant. We have all missed assignments. We were too young in faith to understand the call.

Once, a lady in a Bible study thought that she was supposed to say the word "magnolia" to the group at the end. She felt uncomfortable and doubted she heard right. She passed up the opportunity. Seconds later, at the end of the meeting, another lady spoke up and said, "I don't know why, but I feel I am supposed to say magnolia." A new member of the Bible study began to weep. She explained that her mother's death was still so painful to her and she had asked the Lord to bring her comfort. At her mother's funeral, the magnolia tree blooms reminded her of God's sweetness and care for her pain. She was comforted beyond imagination by the expression. When we miss the assignment, God goes to the next willing soul. As we watch, we learn and grow in knowing the Master's voice.

Cooperate, Don't Lead

It feels cooperative when we are not opening doors but watching them open. We are not setting plans into motion; we are praying God's plan into action. John was working with me on a business deal. John's position was that he had a great plan for us to implement. He requested that I support his plan and count on God to show up. Sadly, we had different understandings of how it was to work. In no way did I think what he was asking me to do was reasonable. Instead of making our own plans and asking God to show up, I was expecting God to provide the plan. As I passed on this work, I watched a $50,000 contract go away. In time, God brought another person from that same company who offered us an excellent contract. My cooperation is with God's plan even if it means upsetting someone around me. God's plans are orderly. They make great sense when they are finally revealed. If what someone is asking you to do is not right in your mind and in your spirit, walk away.

Clarity is the most important part of working in God's timing. When we are unsure, unclear, unconfident, and unconvinced, those are perfect indicators to wait. The Master instructor shows His students the path with clarity. While we are lost in confusion on a matter, we can't act. When we don't feel compelled to act or the action is unclear … wait. Most of the answers He brings are with resources that are right in front of us. When He brings clarity, we can see His cleverness, resourcefulness, and wisdom. The irony of it all is that the unknowing person thinks we have reacted brilliantly, when in fact it was not us at all, but Christ in us. Then we have the joy of giving Him the glory.

Let the Power Flow

We have been promised the *power* of the Holy Spirit. That is a strong word and perfectly chosen by the Father to convey what this resource would be like. The more we serve, the more power we are granted and the more we are understood by His friends and followers. We are told we are in His army. To complete His mission, we must be battle ready. Communication is vital to win wars. In battle, men with the most advanced communication systems can outsmart the enemy. The Germans were the masters of the sea when they used enigma to transmit messages from submarines under the water. Pilots who had sonar communication could sneak up on the enemy without them knowing that they were in enemy territory. For those of you who are sure you know the Master's voice, He will begin to speak to you

When we miss the assignment, God goes to the next willing soul. As we watch, we learn and grow in knowing the Master's voice.

When we are unsure, unclear, unconfident, and unconvinced, those are perfect indicators to wait.

more in codes, in jumbles. The spirit will decipher it to avoid the enemy knowing the battle plan. Get on board. You will have to hear Him to help.

As Christ pulls the line closer to the end of time, He will need laborers in the field who are not concerned about what people of the earth think. He will dress us differently in our skills, and we will stand out as one who is not a part of the earth. Only the strong will be able to work for Him at that point. Christians will then band together more closely, more in agreement to be able to support and encourage each other, since we no longer look and act like the world.

The power that flows from your hands will be more amazing, more vivid, and more intent. As His friends, so are we His disciples. The miracles will amaze you, and they will amaze the world. And just as He has promised in His Word, heard by the disciples hundreds of years ago, so will you know who and what to place your rod upon. Your rod will not be a shaft; it will be a power that is like electric bolts that leave your hand, not visible, but so powerful that the flesh will jump with energy. Arise and march to service. It will no longer be dull or boring to serve Christ. We will begin to clearly see the things that were written clearly in the word. To call upon the faith of a mustard seed really meant to call upon the name of Jesus Christ and you can move mountains. That was meant not literally but figuratively. The mountain you move will be the enemy's camp. Take the mountain. Take the earth for Jesus.

What starts with prayer will end with action. You will be empowered by the Spirit, as you surrender to Him at various levels. You will find that you belong to Him more fully, more completely. He will need all of you—not just your time and money, but your soul's complete commitment to carry out His commission, the Great Commission. We will be disguised as the world as we look like hairdressers, teachers, mothers, workers, and friends. You will then be in places to harvest the fields.

> Then saith he unto his disciples, The harvest truly is plenteous, but the laborers are few (Matt. 9:37).

You will take home the victory in the field. Your field of work is where He will establish you. You will become the best at what you do, to draw the innocent, unknowing into your places. And when you have shared Christ, then they will know why you are the best. You will share more of Christ and less of you. You will be just as John the Baptist did in John 3 when he explained that he was not the Bridegroom but rather the bridegroom's best friend who was happy for the bridegroom.

Christ in you will increase, and you will decrease. Your body will not just be a temple; it will be a camp where the resources for battling the enemy will be stored up. The body will become like a machine equipped to work at the highest levels of action. When He says walk, you walk, rest, you rest, take the hill, you take the hill. Bring your pots empty and let God fill you with new oil. Cleanse your body of the wrong, the hurts, and the obsessions that keep the body from being in optimum performance. Commitments will be stepped up. You will not be able to live in both camps. You will be removed as a traitor if you try to both sleep with the enemy and serve the name of Jesus. But worry not, since the Lord provides all things. The yearning to serve Him will grow too. The choices you make will determine the camp you are in. He gives us freedom of choice in all matters. You will become transparent in the eyes of your fellow servicemen. Your actions and motives will be easily discerned as the ability to discern will be another tool that comes to fullness

Christians will then band together more closely, more in agreement to be able to support and encourage each other, since we no longer look and act like the world.

Your rod will not be a shaft; it will be a power ... not visible, but so powerful that the flesh will jump with energy. Arise and march to service. It will no longer be dull or boring to serve Christ.

for those that make the commitment to do the work His way. It will become more dangerous than ever to not know how to hear Him.

You Have Been Chosen

Take this not in fear. What you have been practicing and preparing for will come. You will find great pleasure in carrying out His orders. Your marksmanship at hitting the target will become more and more accurate. Your height and weight will be measures by the size of your assignment book. Your appearance will be your focus, your form, and your foundation for carrying out the work. In Him, you will find all the comfort you need to enjoy this level of service. Temptations will lessen as you would not give up anything to be removed from His presence. You will find and feel what He meant when Mark 16:15 ESV said, "Go into all the world preaching, teaching and telling the Good News." You are not to wonder if women can do God's work, for God chooses His workers by their willingness to report to duty. He was the first and last not to discriminate. He wrote the policy manual on EEO, accepting all people regardless of race, age, sex, or religious origin. Even Jews will come to know Him as the Messianic Jews come to Him.

And you are not to wonder if women can do God's work ... He chooses His workers by their willingness to report to duty ... He wrote the policy manual on EEO, accepting all people regardless of race, age, sex, or religious origin.

He is the first, the last, the everlasting savior. He is the reason we are here, the reason we are safe, and the reason we can serve without condemnation for our imperfections. We are reminded in Romans 5:8 TLB, while we were yet sinners, He died for us. Not waiting until we were improved, He died first, showing us what He meant when He said, that the greatest gift is love. John 15:13 ESV says, "Greater love hath no man than this, that a man lay down his life for his friends."

He chose us to be in His army, reside in this camp, follow His action plans, and lead lost soldiers back to His side. His Word tells us how the battle ends. He reigns on high. He knows that we will be persecuted, but not forsaken; cast down, but not destroyed. When He completes His work, He will have shared His plan with the whole world. At that point, He will rest knowing that by choice we are His, not by force. Love is a choice. John 15:9 says, "As the Father hath loved me, so have I loved you: continue ye in my love."

A New Life Awaits You!

God desires to lead you, resolve your challenges, furnish your needs, care for your concerns, reward your rightful living, and pour out love into your over stressed, limited trusting world. God said over and over that He desired to bless you. How many more ways can He say this without you letting go and allowing Him to handle the matters of this confusing world.

What's holding you back? How bad do you want to know Him? Where do you go next? In taking time to read this study, God is honored. Take it one step further and glorify Him with your life. Make each day His. Worry less. Trust this living God more.

Relax and allow bigger miracles to flow through you. Release your life into His hand and find a whole new world awaiting you. May the Holy Spirit that already dwells in all Christ's believers be allowed to rise in you! Rein the power of the Holy spirit, as furnished by God the Father to all those who believe in Jesus as savior and accept the fruitful, successful and peaceful life promised throughout His written word in chapters after chapter of the bible.

God reigns above the earth so you may rein in the power on earth made available to you for His glory!

REVIEW & INTROSPECTION

WEEK 13

CHAPTER 13: FRIENDS IN HIGH PLACES

1. Consider your work situation. Are you working in your comfort zone or faithfully "walking in the unknown"? Explain.

   _____

   _____

2. How can you, as a Christian, decrease risk in business or in life in general?

   _____

   _____

3. According to the text, what attribute is vital in order to act when we hear God's voice?

   _____

   _____

4. "God, sometimes I think about You, even when I am not praying." Can you say this is true of your life? Explain.

   _____

   _____

5. What does the text say God will need from you to carry out His Great Commission? Are you willing to offer that up to Him?

   _____

   _____

6. *When we are unsure, unclear, unconfident, and unconvinced, those are perfect indicators to wait.* Have you ever had an instance in your personal life where you felt this way and should have waited? Did you?

   _____

   _____

7. In your own words, describe below what your life will be like when you begin to better hear Him and precisely carry out His orders.

   _____

   _____

Scripture References: *What do these Scriptures mean to you personally?*
Proverbs 8:34–35

John 15:13

Final Bonus:

You have successfully completed this thirteen-week study. Rejoice! Say a special prayer to God asking for the Holy Spirit's help in bringing to your remembrance in the future all that you have learned. Pray that the concepts provided herein will help you to better hear God's voice, stay within His will for you, and fully equip you to work alongside Him in His Great Commission.

RESOURCES

Book References:

Billheimer, Paul E. *Destined for the Throne*. Minneapolis, MN: Bethany House, 1975.

Bishop, Jim. *The Day Lincoln Was Shot*. New York and Evanston: Harper & Row, 1955.

Cohen, Herb. *You Can Negotiate Anything*. New York: Bantana Books, 1982.

Frenchuk, Gary W. *Timeless Wisdom*. Richmond, VA: Cadmus Promotional Print, revised 1995.

Hinn, Benny. *Good Morning Holy Spirit*. Nashville, TN: Thomas Nelson, 1990.

Kempis, Thomas. *The Imitation of Christ*. Dover Thrift Editions.

Stanley, Charles. *His Precious Blood*. Atlanta, GA: In Touch Ministries, Audiotape MH 284, 1994.

JANE BOSTON

"The more power you can handle, the more responsibility that God and man will impart....the more people will look to you to explain your secret weapon: The power of Christ within you."

Author Jane Boston "looks unto Jesus as the author and finisher of her faith" (I Corinthians 3:3) and believes that Jesus wants nothing more than for His people to hear God's Voice, and to move in God's divine timing, through the power of the Holy Spirit within.

It is no coincidence that Jane's book, *Reigning in His Power....a study on the Holy Spirit*, is published during a time of national confusion, economic downturn and season of spiritual powerlessness. According to Jane, faith is about God's people relinquishing control to Him at the crossroads in life and releasing the power of the Holy Spirit within. Jane contends that God's people are not to experience confusion and the pressure of decision-making. Christ in us desires to guide His people with the Truth of His Word, and the light of the Holy Spirit, past the point of confusion. "The more we are able to hear His voice, the better we can step out in faith and thrust ourselves right into the center of His will for our lives," says Jane.

Jane Boston, president of Motivations, Inc., one of the largest providers of continuing education training for physical, occupational, and speech therapists nationwide, a million dollar annual revenue company, with over 1600 hospitals and medical centers in the consortium member network, annually trains over 5000 therapists and holding over 150 training courses in 41 states. Formerly the Executive Director of Hitchcock Rehab Center in Aiken, SC, Jane grew the company from $250,000 annually to $7 million annually in her 15 year tenure. She also steered a $3.7 million capital building campaign building a modern medical rehabilitation facility for the community. Jane has achieved outstanding success both professionally and personally, and she credits her uncanny ability to hear God's voice, as her crowning glory.

"Having started my career as a medical social worker, I am always asking, 'What are the available resources?' ... The Holy Spirit is a great resource given to us as Christians, because it allows us to communicate directly with our Heavenly Father. The more we understand how to walk in continual union throughout the day with the Father, the more we can score at serving and living in God's perfect plan," says Jane.

It is no coincidence that Jane Boston's success in life and in business is directly related to her deep conviction that situations in life don't just present themselves. Rather, Jane believes that God orchestrates plans for His people, with a plan to prosper, not to harm, and plan to give a future and a hope (Jeremiah 29:11 -14)

Jane Boston, friend, through prayer and the guidance of the Holy Spirit, motivates large audiences and inspires those who know her, to humble themselves to discover the life-changing reality of listening to God's Voice through the Holy Spirit. Calm in spirit, articulate, and resourceful Jane has come to see her life as a vehicle of service to others. She uses her gift of administration to offer continuing education courses for medical rehabilitation professionals through Motivations, Inc., supporting Christian events in communities through Motivations Ministries (a nonprofit organization she co-founded), and shares the knowledge of the Holy Spirit through her books and motivational speaking.

Jane Boston, a much sought-after motivator, has been writing and speaking to Christian audiences for ten years. She was highlighted in the February 2007 issue of *Entrepreneur Magazine*. In 2005, she was named "Woman Business Owner of the Year" by the Charlotte chapter of the National Association of Women Business Owners (NAWBO), and has since been featured on various television and radio shows, including *Charlotte Alive*, with Donica Hudson, *The Danny Fontana Show*, and *Homekeepers* with Arthelene Rippy.

The previous edition of her book *Breaking the Silence, the Art of Hearing God's Voice* has been used to raise more than $29,000 for her church. Proceeds from her publications now benefit her nonprofit organization, Motivations Ministries.

Jane has a Master's Degree in Education and a Bachelor's Degree in Social Work. She currently resides in Tega Cay, South Carolina, with Brian, her husband of thirty years, and they have a twenty-one-year-old son, Scott. To contact her, please visit www.janeboston.com or call (803) 802-5454 ext 203. *Reigning in His Power*...a study on the Holy Spirit.